Life's Hills and Valleys

By

Tracey Pizzino

Tracey Pizzino

authorHOUSE®

AuthorHouse™
1663 Liberty Drive, Suite 200
Bloomington, IN 47403
www.authorhouse.com
Phone: 1-800-839-8640

First published by AuthorHouse 1/30/2009

ISBN: 978-1-4208-3576-2 (sc)

Library of Congress Control Number: 2005901819

Printed in the United States of America
Bloomington, Indiana

This book is printed on acid-free paper.

For Brianna and Amanda, I could not
have asked for two better nieces. This is for you.

Also
In memory of my grandparents
Carl, Mary, John, Catherine and to my cousin Jason.
I love and miss you all.

And finally
To my family and friends, without you none of
this would be possible. Thank you for
your support and always believing in me.
I love you.

T.P.

TABLE OF CONTENTS

FRIENDSHIP

A BETTER PERSON 3

TO SAY THANK YOU 4

MORE LIKE A SISTER 5

MEMORIES 7

ACHES AND PAINS 7

LOSING TOUCH 9

WATCH YOU WALK AWAY 10

TOGETHER AGAIN 11

BY THE WAY 13

PUT INTO A LETTER 15

OUR HEARTS WILL ALWAYS HOLD 16

NOTHING TO SHOW 17

NEVER SAY FOREVER 18

THIS IS HOW I SEE THINGS 20

JUST A WORD 21

SAME OLD GAME 22

FRIENDS MAY COME OR GO 23

A MISUNDERSTANDING 24

YOUR TIME WILL COME 26

GOOD LUCK 27

THE PRICE WE HAD TO PAY 28

BONNIE & BECKY 31

MISERY II 33

THANK YOU FOR MY FRIENDS 34

TOTALLY UP TO YOU 36

GOOD-BYE FRIEND 39

SO FAR AWAY 40

THE DOORWAY OF DOUBTS 41

THROUGH THE YEARS 42

AT THIS POINT 44

FRIENDS II 45

I'LL HOLD ON TO OUR FRIENDSHIP..................................46

AS YOU GO AWAY 49

IS THE COST TO HIGH 50

I REFUSE TO SHED A TEAR 52

A FRIEND IN ME 54

ONLY FOR YOURSELF 56

I'VE ALWAYS TRIED TOO HARD 57

I WONDER HOW 59

THINGS TO SAY BEFORE YOU GO 61

MY FINAL GOOD-BYE 63

ANOTHER DAY TO THINK OF YOU 65

DECEMBER 19, 1989 67

HURT IS NOT THE WORD 68

TO YOU I SAY GOOD-BYE 70

JUST US THREE 72

SAY GOOD-BYE TO YOU 73

YOUR FRIEND 75

I'LL ALWAYS BE HERE 76

LEAVING AGAIN 78

A FRIEND SO TRUE 79

WE MISS YOU 81

SO SORRY 82

THE NICEST ONE 84

NOT THE GREATEST OF FRIENDS 85

DIFFERENCES THAT NEVER CAME 86

LIVE IN TODAY 87

TO ALL OF YOU 89

SORRY IS IN ORDER 90

WHY NOW 94

TWO MONTHS LATER 95

FRIEND IN ME 97

ALWAYS STAYED FRIENDS 98

I DON'T KNOW WHAT TO SAY 99

ME AND YOU BEST FRIENDS 100

NEVER ALONE 103

NOTHING'S WRONG 105

A FRIENDSHIP CAKE 106

JUST REMEMBER FOREVER 108

THIS IS THE DAY 109

TELL ME, TELL ME 111

FRIENDS 112

JUST REMEMBER 114

GOOD FRIENDS 115

DREAMS 116

TO A VERY GOOD FRIEND 117

THANK YOU SO MUCH 118

FOR A SPECIAL FRIEND 120

FALLING APART 120

MY BEST FRIEND 122

TIL DEATH DO US PART 123

CAN YOU PICTURE 125

I WONDER IF... 126

THIS ONE'S FOR YOU 127

WHAT WILL HAPPEN TO OUR FRIENDSHIP..................129

THIS TIME I KNOW 130

SPECIAL 132

DRUG DEALER 133

SYMBOLIZES 134

NO MATTER WHAT 135

ALL BECAUSE OF YOU 136

FRIENDSHIP 137

WHAT IS A BEST FRIEND 138

ONLY TIME CAN TELL 138

IT IS OVER 139

LETTING GO 140

I DON'T HATE HER 141

FEBRUARY 23, 1987 143

THE END RESULT 144

TOO MANY FACES 145

THE TRUE MEANING 147

YOU ARE 149

TO GOOD TO LAST 150

AT THE START 152

MY FRIEND 154

GOOD-BYE 154

YOU ARE THERE 155

WHY GOD GAVE US FRIENDS 156

JUST A FRIEND 156

BEST FRIEND FOREVER 157

A FRIEND 157

THE FRIENDSHIP YOU GAVE ME 158

OPINIONS 159

DIDN'T WANT TO SAY GOOD-BYE 160

IT'S NOT 161

WE MAY HAVE OUR DIFFERENCES 162

TO ME, FRIENDS ALWAYS 163

SUCH GOOD FRIENDS 164

THE HIGHEST COST 165

MY FRIEND AND ME 167

A FRIEND LIKE YOU 167

FOREVER FRIENDS 170

FRIENDS, FOREVER 171

ARE WE STILL FRIENDS 172

SORRY I FORGOT 173

I CAN REMEMBER 174

FRIENDS ARE FOREVER 174

SO, MY FRIEND 175

FRIENDS AGAIN 176

WE THOUGHT YOU WERE OUR FRIEND 176

LET GO OF YOU 177

I DOUBT WE ARE FRIENDS 177

WILL THINGS BE BACK TO NORMAL 178

NOT A SOUND 179

PAUL 180

MY FRIENDS 181

BEYOND ALL DOUBT 184

SUMMER 184

FRIEND GOOD-BYE 185

I WILL NEVER FORGET YOU 186

COUNT ON ME 187

ENDS A DIFFERENT WAY 188

LOVE, MARRIAGE AND BABIES

BRIGHTEN MY DAY 193

MY LAST THOUGHT 194

EVEN IF IT'S NOT ME 195

YOUR LOVE 197

THERE AND BACK 197

IF THINGS WERE MEANT TO BE 199

LET'S NOT FIGHT 200

WITH YOU I LONG TO BE 200

STILL ALONE … 201

I DO 202

JULY 16, 1994 204

TOGETHER ALWAYS STAY 205

A WEDDING DAY WISH 206

TWO HEARTS 207

BABY TO BE 207

CONGRATULATIONS 209

SARAH 210

DECEMBER 2, 1993 211

AMANDA 212

LOSS OF A LOVED ONE

MISSED, MORE THAN YOU KNOW 217

WE SHALL NEVER FORGET YOU 218

JASON 219

JUST A LITTLE WHILE 221

GRAMMA 222

GOOD-BYE MY FRIEND 223

HAVING TO SAY GOOD-BYE 224

GRANDMA 226

UNTIL WE MEET AGAIN 226

GRANDPA 228

MY TIME...228

BIRTHDAYS

WHAT ARE FRIENDS 233

TO YOU, FROM ME 233

ALWAYS THERE 235

FOR A SPECIAL FRIEND ON HER BIRTHDAY 236

HAPPY BIRTHDAY 237

FRIENDS FOREVER 237

A BIRTHDAY THOUGHT 238

HAPPY BIRTHDAY SIS 239

THANK YOU 241

SOMETHING I'D LIKE TO SAY 242

TO YOU FROM ME 243

A SPEICAL PLACE 245

OCTOBER 14, 1993 247

JUST THREE WORDS 248

A WORD SAID SO FREQUENTLY 250

NO AMOUNT OF GOLD 251

A BETTER FRIEND 253

THE PERFECT GIFT 255

A BIRTHDAY WISH 256

MISCELLANEOUS

M.M.I. 261

MOM, WITH LOVE 262

DAD 263

A PROTECTIVE SISTER 264

THINKING OF ME 265

OLD TRICKS NEW SHOES ALL YOU JERKS ARE STUPID
FOOLS 266

JUST BLACK 267

33766 OR 53666 268

STEPS OF AN ADDICT 269

THE HEARTBREAK KID 270

OCEAN 271

BELIEVE 272

LIFE LONG FRIEND 273

CHRISTMAS 1997 274

MERRY CHRISTMAS 276

CLASS OF "88" 277

THIS DAY 278

GRADUATION DAY 279

ALONG THE ROAD 280

CLASS OF "91" 281

YOUR GRADUATION DAY 283

JUST A THOUGHT AWAY 284

FRIENDSHIP

A BETTER PERSON

For all the things you've given me, all the times you cared,
For all the times you put up with me and the memories shared.

For never giving up on me when others walked away,
For always knowing exactly what to say.

To always be willing to listen again and again,
When I was hurt or let down by one of my friends.

To say thank you would be unfair for all you have done for me,
Words cannot even start to explain what it is I see.

A friendship built so stable and strong,
One that could never go wrong.

A person on whom I shall always confide,
To someone who always stood by my side.

For the part of my life you helped change and grow,
I'll always be thankful for, I hope you know.

I am a better person because of you,
Always remember this is true.

And even though we will be miles away,
In my heart Ricky, you shall always stay.

Tracey Pizzino

TO SAY THANK YOU

Something's are taken for granted, without a thought or a care,
Something that one overlooks, yet not everyone can share.

People use the word so carelessly, for everyone they know,
Yet, I don't see it that way, and I'd like to tell you so.

The word I am referring to is "friend" you see,
So this is how I believe it should really be.

It takes a certain person to measure up and fit,
Someone not to funny, but has a certain wit.

A person you can trust, beyond any doubt,
These are the kind of people we can't live without.

Sometimes problems occur, and we must say good-bye,
But friends can overcome this, yet still tears we cry.

It takes special people to affect who we are,
Some signs are obvious, yet some are very far.

But no matter the way they changed us, we tend to forget,
To thank them for what they've done, and that we do regret.

So for everything you have done, I would like to say,
Thank you, I appreciate it, on this special day.

You may not know what I mean or what you did to change,
But my life has a part in which, you helped rearrange.

To say thank you for being my friend, just would not do,
You are more like a sister to me in which I always knew.

I hope you reach your goals and have a future as bright as can be,
And know that no matter what happens, you'll have a friend in me.

I found the meaning of a friend, a little while ago,
And you taught me that, which I hope you know.

I appreciate all you have done for me, always seeing me through,
But most of all, above all else, thanks for being you.

MORE LIKE A SISTER

Things don't always work out the way we think will be,
Me and you friends, people couldn't see.

But prove them wrong we did, beyond any doubt,
And no matter how badly, neither one of us ever backed out.

We have bad days like all other friends,
Yet never once did we let it end.

For our good times just couldn't compare,
To the arguments in which we both shared.

From Michigan to Florida and back again,
Through it all we remained friends.

Tracey Pizzino

I shall miss working with you, but even more,
I shall miss the talks like we had before.

No more going to the bar just on a whim,
No more saying, no he said that, him.

No more spur of the moment things,
Like tonight your clothes from home bring.

You are staying the night, don't drive that far,
We'll go to Dave's instead of the bar.

But above all else, one thing I can tell,
As friends we turned out pretty well.

And for those who just couldn't see,
The likeness between you and me.

Must not have been looking in the right places,
For they will have to go much deeper than just our faces.

And look to the center of our hearts and minds,
For a friendship like ours, is rare to find.

For when you think back at the times gone by,
I hope there will be a smile and not a sigh.

And for whatever other reason for us to have met,
One thing I hope you will never forget.

You are not only a person I work with now and then,
You are more like a sister and a very good friend.

MEMORIES

The memories I have are with me to stay,
No matter how you act or what you say.

For they are with me each step of the day,
And that is one thing you can't take away.

I will never forget the memories of the fun,
For we had lots of them in the sun.

All the tennis and the talks,
The crying and the taking walks.

The days we all talked to each other,
For all of you were like my brother.

Maybe in time the memories won't hurt so bad,
Or when at times of recall make me sad.

ACHES AND PAINS

To stop waiting around will still take a lot,
But sooner or later you guys I will have forgot.

Tracey Pizzino

We did have fun times while it did last,
But all you guys are now in my past.

I am finally listening to my friends,
To clean the slate and start over again.

I'm through with all the aches and pains,
But most of all playing your games.

I will never let myself be hurt again,
And think that you are a good friend.

But now I have to forget it at last,
And live in the future, not in the past.

The memories will always be there, that we all shared,
But it is still hard to believe that you once cared.

I have to forget it, that would be best,
And try to put all the bad memories to rest.

But even with good memories at times of recall,
I would rather not remember you at all.

Because of the hurt, aches and pains,
But most of all, all your games.

I hate to say good-bye, but it's something I must do,
I must forget the past, but most of all you.

LOSING TOUCH

How can I put this, so you won't get mad?
It's something that's true, yet still sad.

You are all so worried about losing touch,
But trust me it doesn't really mean that much.

You will have your friends at college, to hang around then,
You won't even think twice of me my friend.

We always had a good time, all of us together,
But we didn't promise it would be like this forever.

Changes occur good and bad, there is nothing we can do,
Just try and remember the friends we knew.

That's all we can ask, and pray the others try,
To keep everyone together, to not say good-bye.

But let's face the fact; losing touch is how it will end,
Because you guys don't like to write, not now, not then.

So it's only a matter of time, before it falls apart,
And with it we'll all lose a small piece of our heart.

Losing touch I'll try my hardest not to do,
But part of this responsibility also falls on you.

Tracey Pizzino

WATCH YOU WALK AWAY

What am I to do, what am I to say,
When it is time for you to go away.

Will it be the same and grow with each passing year,
Or will it just be wiped away like a first tear.

Will it be listed as just one of those things and all,
Tell me what will happen should you I call.

Will you brush it off like you did right now,
Or will you try to contact me somehow.

Well I guess I know what the answer is going to be,
 It's not going to be the same between you and me.

You are going to make new friends, yet will you forget the old,
Or will your heart be able to always hold.

All of the memories, the letters and stuff,
The good times and even the day's things got rough.

Tell me will it be the same like before you went away,
Or will you have nothing more to say.

Should I prepare myself to say good-bye forever?
And talk to you again, never.

I have a feeling that's what it is going to come to,
For you will move on to something new.

I just hope when the day finally arrives, I will be able to say,
Good-bye, good luck and then walk away.

For I must let go of a friendship so carefully and yet,
Pray and hope that me you don't forget.

But should that ever happen just please always know,
I'll always pray and hope you're safe no matter where you go.

I hope you do well, I'll pray for only the best,
And when the day comes I'll pray you pass the tests.

But now there's nothing more for me to do and nothing more to say, I'll just have to stand by quietly and watch you walk away.

TOGETHER AGAIN

Here we are together again,
And this time we are going to stay friends.

No more fighting, no more lies,
Nothing to regret and no reason to cry.

Maybe we won't talk everyday,
Maybe we won't have anything to say.

But at least we will part when the time comes around,
And we will never let the other one down.

Tracey Pizzino

Things were going good, but then went wrong,
One of us always is trying to stay strong.

Well I won't be the same; I promise this to you,
No more will I try to tell you what to do.

Even if we don't talk, at least we will stay,
Friends forever together today.

I won't say sorry and I won't hit for fun,
I won't always be willing to say what was done.

I'll mind my own business on that I will end,
Because for once things are fine and we are again friends.

Well now I am done, I guess there is nothing more,
So I will just leave and close the door.

The past is just that and that is where it shall stay,
Even if it means me walking away.

So in all, the phrase "together again" doesn't only say,
That we must see or talk to each other everyday.

In fact just the opposite it is always that when,
We keep our distance, we still remain friends.

Everything is over and done with, my attitude is gone,
I know that I am right do you still think I am wrong?

Well there it is, us together again,
And this is the best way for us to stay friends.

BY THE WAY

Though the best of friends we may not always be,
But friends we are you and me.

Something's have changed from good to bad, and back again,
But one thing that shall always be, the three of us friends.

Sure we may have had bad days, which turned into years,
And yes with those I shall admit I shed a lot of tears.

But one thing that I owe you, more than anything else,
Is you taught me how to better myself.

You taught me how to handle things whether right or wrong,
And how I can stand up to anything and still remain strong.

I have learned to accept the truth whether good or bad,
To understand it's better than lies, even if it makes you sad.

To set a line or limit myself to not always be so nice and yet,
To always put credit where credit is due, I never would forget.

You all may have taught me the hard way, and yes painful at times,
But old friends are the wiser ones and very hard to find.

Tracey Pizzino

I have a standard that I live by, where my friends are concerned,
This is something I did not inherit, but something that I learned.

I'd rather not be someone's friend by honestly, then stay their
friend by lies,
And that standard I owe to all of you guys.

I maybe very dumb at times, but you knew that to be true,
And I always forgave people, and that I still do.

But the past is over and the present is at hand,
The future I won't think about, or try to understand.

I just wanted to let you know, that because of the past I'm better,
No matter how bad the situation, no matter what the weather.

I see this in a different way, then I did before,
I can confront things, I am not afraid anymore.

Thank you all once again and oh by the way,
I'll never forget any of you or what you did say.

My friends you are no matter the reason,
Always there no matter the season.

The best is hard to find, even harder to see,
So how in the hell did I find you three?

PUT INTO A LETTER

A letter is more than a simple hello, or even a good-bye,
It may be intended to make people smile or to make them cry.

To let someone know everything's fine, or something is very wrong,
To tell a friend it's okay, and together you'll stay strong.

To let them know how you feel, to tell them that you care,
Something that will always be around, when you can't be there.

Something to remind them of you and how you see things to be,
Nothing more than communication between you and me.

It enables you at any moment to recall the good and bad,
Words that are often encouraging should you become sad.

But most important above anything else, a letter lets you think things out,
When you are having problems or even having doubts.

They are always there in the shape of a note, card or letter,
Something to make you smile and cry makes everything seem better.

So even if things go wrong and friends move on through,
What they have left behind are memories and feelings that were true.

Nothing of elegance, nothing of steel,
Just some friendships that are so real.

Tracey Pizzino

Letters are so much more complicated then they really seem,
For you must dissect and take them apart, then the lines read between.

For this is the best way I have seen, believe it or not,
To reassure one of your friends, that them you haven't forgot.

Whether you were mad at them or whatever,
The memories and feelings are best said when put into a letter.

OUR HEARTS WILL ALWAYS HOLD

Things were going good; everything was on track like it should be,
But now the future is so hard to see.

Everyone is going to be leaving and going on their way,
I have a funny feeling there will be nothing more to say.

Sure we can promise until our face is blue,
But what will happen, it won't come true.

Maybe at first we will keep in touch,
Then just a few times every other month.

Finally it will all stop and where will we be,
No longer will it be everyone, not even just three.

But we all must grow-up and I guess grow apart too,
But don't think for a minute I will forget any of you.

Never a dull moment, but now they will be memories in the end,
Because we must prepare ourselves to say good-bye to friends.

But I shall fight until I can't fight anymore,
I'll never give up or shut the door.

I'll try to stay in touch until summers back again,
That's when we will all be back together as friends.

I know the distance will not change the past, and the future can't
be told,
I just hope the love from our friendships our hearts will always
hold.

NOTHING TO SHOW

We had a group, with so many friends,
But now I am sorry to say it did end.

We went separate ways, a little at a time,
The friends we hung around with, we can no longer find.

We all have doubts as to what happened and why,
When was the point when we could no longer cry?

Everything was good, nothing too bad,
No one was hurt, no one was sad.

Everyone was happy; we all had a blast,
But all of that is just a thing of the past.

Nothings the same, nothing at all,
We can't even pick each other up when we fall.

Things fell apart and the pieces are too scattered around,
In a million pieces all over the ground.

Too many to pick up and put back together,
Not even enough time to say forever.

We will never let anything get in the way,
That is what all of us at one point did say.

Well things got in the way and the result in the end,
Is all of us together, just barely friends.

I tried to hold on as tight as I could,
But as you can see it didn't do that much good.

I guess things have ended, and with nothing to show,
But it's finally time for me to let it go.

NEVER SAY FOREVER

Who should we turn to, what do we do,
I think of this every night through.

Will things work out so we can see?

What finally happened between you and me?

Or is this another case of something that went wrong,
A friendship that was very stable and so strong.

But the strongest of things can be torn apart,
When lost is the slightest of hearts.

Never say forever, for forever is too far away,
And it has no meaning for me today.

Because how can we promise something where no one has ever been,
It's stupid to call people your forever friend.

But to have a friend for life or longer is what I want to be,
That's all I ask of you and me.

But I guess it's time to come back to reality, the present is here,And it's everything I ever did fear.

How can people have so much fun, then have it fade away with time?
That's what happened with some friends of mine.

Everything is crazy, but I did learn a thing or two,
About what to say and what not to do.

Don't look too far into the future for no one knows what's to be,
I just hope in the days to come, together is all of you and me.

All we can do now is hope, pray and try,
To never say forever for that makes me cry.

THIS IS HOW I SEE THINGS

Even though you're feeling down,
And your friends are not around.
You're thinking you are all alone,
Because you are away from home.
That no one listens and no one cares,
Because no one is right there.
Just think back to the happy times and always smile,
You'll be back home in a little while.
But when things look hard on the road ahead,
Or you're beat and you dread.
Another day in the heat and sun,
Just remember you've already won.
Just think of it has a test,
And only give it your best.
There's another way to look at it though,
Think of it as friend or foe.
The biggest risk of all in life,
Is the word friendship, it's full of strife.
If you can survive all the pain it brings,
And then you find a friend who does not use strings.
That's when you found a friendship that's very stable and strong,
One that will last through time and be there if you're wrong.
But let's keep it simple, this is how I see,
The friendship that exists between you and me.

JUST A WORD

Things are good, and then go bad,

At times so happy, others sad.

Things are everything you could ever need,

Then that feeling on which you feed.

To belong, to fit in with your friends,

You think that it's only the end.

You are the only person, who wants to better yourself,

It's dumb and stupid to everyone else.

Yet the names don't stop and the tears still flow,

And you are still the one who is stupid though.

The effects of a little word or a phrase said,

Stops us from living and pronounces us dead.

For at that moment it's where we want to be,

Nothing to harm us, no one to see.

Then again things are bright and a new day has begun,

And this day is like the rest, we must conquer until it's won.

Some days it's easy, other times it is hard,

To always walk around never put down your guard.

I have tried so many times to ignore it day to day,

But it gets to where we only hear what the others say.

When someone talks to you, you think what he knows inside,

Then another time comes for us to run and hide.

Friends don't understand the strength this burden bears,

And how many people that this way of thinking is shared.

I've looked over most of what has happened in the past,

But one thing remains, my memory will last.

All the bad things ever said or done lingers in my mind,

Said by friends the rarest of kinds.

Maybe they meant it in a different way,

But it is easier for me to believe all the bad people say.

When you hear it for so long, that's what you believe,

There is nothing for me, I'll never achieve.

But my future I am building and all I see is bright,

I'll prove them all wrong and make everything right.

For the support I have gotten from all of my friends,

I would like to thank you once again.

To the ones who hated my decisions, yet still stood by my side,

It's because of you, I no longer must hide.

Everyone whom I have known through the good, bad, and pain,

It's that alone that's kept me sane.

Thank you for everything, for which you have done,

Because this is a battle I have indeed won.

SAME OLD GAME

Things are so hard to see,

First of all how can this be?

I was thinking the same as you,

But both too dumb to see it through.

To ask the other were you mad,

Instead I sat here oh so sad.

Wondering was any of it real,

Or was it just what I thought, a deal.

To have such a good friend, was to hard to believe,

After all that was said, with nothing up your sleeve.

I have to talk this out with you, put everything on the table,
To once and for all see if our friendship is stable.

To find out the truth to a question at hand,
Something I need to really understand.

Am I going to regret once more,
Me opening the same old door.

Was I right to call you again,
Believing that we are still friends.

FRIENDS MAY COME OR GO

Some friends may come, some may go, but very few may stay,
You learn a lot from those who leave, or simply walk away.

The lesson may have helped or hurt, it's a risk we all face,
And in that group there's always those, no one can take their place.

Sometimes things are oh so clear, but we chose not to see,
What the problems may have been and what should be.

Things just go from bad to worse; there is no good in sight,
I am so tired of trying to figure out wrong from right.

My friends I guess are just that, in my heart friends they'll stay,
But I am sick of getting hurt, so I must walk away.

It will be hard, like you said, for I am not mean at all,
But I'm so tired of picking myself up each time they make me fall.

Things are bound to get better, believe me this I know,
It will just take sometime, like the melting of the snow.

And one day I'll be friends again, with those whom went away,
But until then I just have to take it day to day.

Thank you very much for understanding and just being there,
It's so nice to know I have a brother-friend who really cares.

You have helped me a lot and one day I'll return the favor you'll see,
I will be the kind of friend to you, which you have been to me.

A MISUNDERSTANDING

I don't know why I can't let go, why is that to be,
Why can't I understand, why can't I see.

They say you can only let go of something that meant nothing at the start,
Well this friendship started with all heart.

Something was misunderstood I don't know how or why,
But all my tears are long since gone, I can no longer cry.

I would talk to you again at the drop of a hat, but that I just can't
do,
I have a feeling this one disagreement we won't make it through.

I mailed you a letter explaining my side of things between us
two,Not once did I ever hear from you.

How do you think of this, do you even want to talk,
Or would you like me to find a short peer, and then take a long
walk.

Some say time will heal this, and talking again we'll be,
How when friends again, me and you is so hard to see.

I'll wait how long it takes and should forever roll my way,
That's the time we'll be friends, but when I cannot say.

Please don't think I hate you, because it's just not true,
And don't think for just one minute I never missed you.

Because everyday things remind me of how it use to be,
The happy and bad times between you and me.

To have those days back again, I'd give my life away,
Just to be able to talk to you, to see what you'd say.

But I'll never know what I did to make you want to end,
The fact that me and you were really good friends.

Take care of yourself and please always know,
The hardest part will be, if you decide to let go.

Tracey Pizzino

YOUR TIME WILL COME

I don't know how to start, but this is for myself,

Though others may read it, it is for me and no one else.

My thought and my feelings, my hopes and my dreams,

And all my heartaches that gathered between.

Two people I thought of as the best at one time,

Friends I thought the rarest to find.

I really can't say how things fell apart,

I can't even pinpoint when it did start.

The only thing I know for sure, I gave it my best,

But no matter how good that was, I never passed the test.

I told them how I saw things and how it made me feel,

But now all I do is wonder, was any of it real.

Will I ever know why things went this way?

Will they have the courage to talk to me and say?

That they messed up or they want it to end,

That there is no point for us to continue being friends.

Maybe they are thinking the opposite too,

And still want to be friends and see this through.

But I can't stop time and figure out what's right,

For the days only grow longer then turn to night.

The one thing I am wondering, if something should go wrong,

Will the memories keep them going strong?

Will they ever know how much I did care?

Could they understand how much, I wanted to be there.

If this was a first time thing, I'd look over it in a glance,

But this I believe is their third chance.

And every time I go back and apologize to them two,

But this time sorry, no can do.

I've done my share of apologizing and my feelings are so clear,

Both of you know your friendships were very dear.

But how can I hold onto something when you don't give me the time,

The friends I cared so much for I can no longer find.

I have treated both of you the best, and I deserve much better,

And to you it didn't mean anything the poem or the letter.

You'll always be a part of my memories and my past,

But I have to say good-bye and move on at last.

If a second chance comes around again,

I'd have to say I'm sorry; it has already reached the end.

I will never wish you harm, that I'll never say,

But for what you've done to me, I hope one day you'll pay.

And someone you care about decides to turn and go,

And an explanation why they left, that you'll never know.

Then and only then will you know the pain I've gone through,

But it won't be on me this time; it will all be on you.

GOOD LUCK

You have been there through the good times and the tears,
I feel like I have known you forever, not only three years.

You always had a way of putting a smile on my face,
Always putting me in my place.

You always knew exactly what to say,
But as for now it's a brand new day.

And away you must go,
To insure your future this I know.

You will be missed more than words can explain,
But you won't see me throwing a guilt trip or placing blame.

It is something I know you must do,
And I will be sad when I say bye to you.

But for everything you have taught me one thing I know,
You will always be in my thoughts no matter where you go.

So before I end this I would like to add,
That the memories of our friendship will never make me sad.

For when the time comes and you I recall,
I will remember you with a smile or not at all.

For in my heart you have been,
Not only a co-worker but also my friend.

THE PRICE WE HAD TO PAY

I wonder if you do care,
Do you know that I'm not there?

I wonder, do you recall,
The promise you made that day and all.

Will I regret talking to you again?
Thinking you are my friend.

No you said, straight as you can be,
To my face, you lied to me.

Do you think of the good old days?
When all we did was laugh and play.

Do you wonder at all, sometimes?
What's going on in my mind?

Do you comprehend the effects and sighs?
The hurt if you say good-bye.

The wondering I've done at night,
Trying to separate wrong from right.

Understanding what I did,
Thinking who was I trying to kid.

I wonder how things would have been,
Should we have stayed good friends?

We started out as great ones, but then that changed,
From good to okay, to barely sane.

If things were differently then they are today,
Would you still have gone the other way?

Are you waiting for me to call you?
If so, that I will not do.

Tracey Pizzino

Because I am waiting for you to call me,
If I have to wait forever, that's how long it will be.

You have hurt me more than once or twice,
And I only have for you, advice.

I treated you the best as with everyone else,
And the only person you thought of was yourself.

I never asked for anything, but the one thing that you lost,
Our friendship, I had to pay with the highest cost.

You decided to let it go, without even a blink,
You didn't really care what the hell I would think.

Well thank you for assuming and hurting me too,
And I do regret talking again to you.

But before I end this, I still would like to know,
Why is it that you had to let go.

That's one of many questions I'll never have the answer for,
The only thing I can recall is the shutting of the door.

I wonder if you ever think if I'm fine or dead,
The one thing I'd like to know, what is in your head?

Do you care how your actions have affected me?
You could not have hurt me more, if you'd hung me from a tree.

But I could ask myself questions and think how it could have been,
But why put myself through hell, when you don't even want to be friends.

And I'm not blaming you, so don't blame me,
It's just one of those things that weren't meant to be.

And if it ever was, we stopped trying along the way,
And as the end result, we both had to pay.

Our friendship was the price, unfortunate but true,
But no matter what has happened, I shall miss you.

One of us stopped caring, some time ago,
Which one it was, that we'll never know.

BONNIE & BECKY

How I met you two was strange, the circumstances and all,
Then suddenly one day each other we decided to call.
Every now and then we'd talk, should we see the other one,
But never did I ever dream two friendships had begun.
But they just grew and time made them strong,
And my friendship with both of you could never be wrong.
Now here we are today and months have passed by,
Pieces that just fell together we never had to try.
Well now that I have your attention,
There is something I'd like to mention.
You have both been good to me, and there's no doubt in my mind,
That our friendship is strong and stable and will last through time.

Becoming my friend is easy, but staying my friend is hard,

But with you two by my side, I can put down my guard.

This friendship is a two way street, with rights and lefts too,

Always giving each other the chance to better me and you.

Leaving options open to everything in sight,

Never saying a certain person is always wrong or right.

I really can't say how things would go,

As light as rain or as heavy as snow.

With you both for me to call, if I need a friend to care,

Two people I can always talk to, and who's always there.

So Bonnie and Becky, I dedicate this poem for you,

For all the times you've helped me through.

But should the day arrive when I'm no longer around,

Maybe because I have moved or I am under ground.

I'll never forget either of you, because of the joy and the laughter,

Will always remind me, I received the best for now and ever after.

I'll never be sad when I think back and see,

All the memories of you and me.

Because it's not what we haven't seen or even what we've heard,

It doesn't even have to be the simplest of words.

It's just the memory, etched forever in my mind,

Of two of the best friends I'll ever find.

I'll never be able to thank you for everything you see,

For the kindness and friendship I've given to others, you've given back to me.

So should the distance grow between us and days should turn to years,

Our friendships will not have one worry and never shed a tear.

Because even if we are not in reach of the others hand,

In my mind I know, together the three of us will stand.

MISERY II

Things were kind of crazy today,
It's kind of hard to really say.

Everything was going great to start,
Then things just fell apart.

Shopping was good, in fact fine,
Then after came the time.

For everything to go as wrong as could be,
And the only people mad were Bonnie and me.

I was being nice and to a movie we saw,
Bonnie, Dave, Mickey and me, all.

Bonnie bought us stuff to eat,
We were acting anything but beat.

Then to Mickey's house we did go,
Driving slowly through the snow.

We were all downstairs not talking to anyone,
Not saying anything of what we've done.

Mickey playing Nintendo, then Dave shutting the door,
Leaving me and Bonnie sitting on the floor.

So we got up to leave, and say good-bye,
But Dave shut the door, why even try.

So to Bonnie's house we did drive,
So mad and hurt, what they did was jive.

Yet when we called Mickey's it was on us they place the blame,
Well look sweethearts were holding the flame.

And we are not the ones, who are going to get burned,
One day this I hope you will learn.

I maybe your friend till the end you see,
Even though you have hurt me.

So be mad if you must, I don't quite care,
Because you know if you need me I'll be there.

But I'm not going to apologize, so don't hold your breath long,
Cause this time we are right and you two are wrong.

THANK YOU FOR MY FRIENDS

I don't know how to handle this, not even what to say,
Things were always fine, and then it slipped away.
The friendship we had was the best I thought,
Until you decided to take it apart.
You could have done it differently then the way you did chose,
Because you're the only one who's going to lose.
I put everything into this friendship at hand,
Why is that so hard for you to understand?
I went to the games and stopped by,

But it seemed from your end, you just didn't want to try.

I trusted you with everything and talked to you too,

Now you just up and left me blue.

Well my blue mood has changed and my skies are clear,

And for you, in my eyes, there is not one tear.

My crying days are over, when I think of the past,

And my friendship with you has taught me a lesson that will last.

You can't judge a person by what you have heard or seen,

The lines you must take apart and read between.

I won't forget the good times, and with those come the bad,

I won't even say that it only made me sad.

But I can't just look at the good parts, but it as a whole,

And I can't believe I fell into this friendship heart and soul.

I can't say I'll accept this back with open arms, if it's to be,

Because us being friends is just too hard to see.

This is not the way I wanted things to go,

I'll always care and think of you that I hope you know.

Even the silence I could have accepted, that's not the case,

It's mostly the day you laughed in my face.

It was all a joke to you, why I was mad,

You couldn't see you hurt me or made me sad.

All you were thinking of was you,you,you,

It didn't matter who you made blue.

I hope you come to realize the effects of your actions,

And their out comes live up to your satisfaction.

It's not that I didn't try, because God knows I did,

You just have to grow up and stop acting like a kid.

So before I go I'd like to say just a word or two,

There is one thing, I'd like to thank you.

For all the people I talk to now,

Because I met them through knowing you somehow.

Tracey Pizzino

TOTALLY UP TO YOU

I'm not asking you for reasons, or saying it's a plan,
I'm not trying to judge, but to simply understand.

Why things are going the way they are,
I've been sitting back and looking but only from a far.

Well I kind of got to close and I saw what I feared,
Then I left your house and then came the tears.

But they stopped as soon as they did start,
Because I realized I was taking this to heart.

I have to stop and think about things you see,
It's not at all the same between you and me.

I know you are busy and have hardly any time at all,
And you have not one minute to pick up a phone and call.

But the letters are different; they're as simple as they may,
I wrote you two, did you throw them away.

You told me you did not read one, that's really clear,
Do you really want to or don't you even care.

I bought you a card to say things are fine,
But this one day you didn't take the time.

Of course you read it, but not one thought in sight,
Not even an expression to say I'm wrong or right.

Then the phone rang and you talked for a while,
Then a frown took the place of my smile.

As I listened to you talk on the phone, I could see and hear,
Things between you and me are no longer clear.

When I talk to you on the phone or even face to face,
Things were always good and there never was a space.

But now that little space as turned to a long and silent pause,
What I thought of as a great friendship suddenly has 100 flaws.

When I ask a question the only thing you say,
Is a simple one word answer that slowly fades away.

I don't want this to end, but my trying is done,
I can't hold onto a friendship, when there really isn't one.

I've tried so hard to help and understand the what's and why's,
But I'm just too fed up and I don't want to try.

I've told you how I see things in words and to your face,
I have also told you no one could take your place.

When everyone started saying things I didn't want to hear,
I came to you instead of facing my fears.

I told you I would accept the fact that they had lied not you,
That you were the one who was telling the truth.

Tracey Pizzino

I've never jumped to conclusions, and I don't want to start now,
But I have to do something, someway, somehow.

I'm going to stop right here and not go on any more,
Because I can't stand to knock and have you shut the door.

As I have said before my trying days are through,
The cards I have turned over now my friend to you.

It's your turn to do what ever you see right,
You can let the days shine, or make dim the light.

You can say it's over, the friendship at hand,
Or you can talk to me and make me understand.

But I will not call you until you make a choice,
To call or talk is when I'll hear your voice.

I won't go to any games or stop by your house,
I'll go my own way; I'll be as quiet as a mouse.

So however this turns out, for the good, bad, or same,
One thing I know for certain, where not to place the blame.

And though my tears may start to fall and my skies turn blue,
The fate of our friendship I leave totally up to you.

GOOD-BYE FRIEND

No matter what the name badge said, you treated us the same,
You never just pointed a finger at someone to place the blame.

No matter what needed to be done, you always asked instead,
Of just telling people what to do, then tilt back your head.

And to my recall you never looked down on us a bit,
You always made me feel like here I did fit.

Sure you had your bad days, which I've had mine too,
But you always seemed to help me make it through.

Willing to listen to all of the complaints I had,
And there you were making me smile when I was sad.

Working with you was great; you were one of the best,
You worked hard to reach where you are, you only deserve the best.

So with whatever lies in front of you, I hope you will know,
I'll pray for your success no matter where you go.

And though you are leaving one thing will always be,
No one can take away what you have taught me.

Now I don't want to make you sad, for your last day has reached the end,
But I shall miss you lots, and think of you my friend.

Tracey Pizzino

SO FAR AWAY

One day you were here, the next day gone,

Everything was right, yet something wrong.

You had no time to say good-bye,

You had to get packed, and then fly.

And even though you are far away,

In my thoughts you shall stay.

Though I am sad and miss you friend,

Things will be worth it in the end.

You are doing this for your future to be,

And no one is prouder than me,

You had the courage to up and go,

To only better a person I know.

But to have you not here, is strange I will say,

For I can't call you up, and tell you I'm coming over today.

I have not seen you in a while but yet,

Our friendship will grow, you can bet.

No matter how long you are there,

I hope you know I still care.

I will not lie and tell you things are okay,

And that I wasn't hurt when I found out you left the other day.

But I do understand the reason,

Sort of like the change of season.

But when it is time they come back once more,

But always better than before.

And even though time has passed us by,

There is no need for me to cry.

You will be back sooner than I know,

I just hope we have time to talk before you have to go.

Away to school, college to be more precise,

I just hope things go smoothly and nice.
Then again I'll have to say good-bye to you,
Something I'll hate to do.
But things could be worse then they are today,
At least you are coming home and not staying so far away.
But there are two more things I'd like to mention,
So listen close and pay attention.
I can't grant you a wish or make miracles come true,
Yet I can't pretend everything's fine and that I don't miss you.
But one thing I can promise you, you must always remember,
No amount of miles can change the fact you are my friend forever.

THE DOORWAY OF DOUBTS

Worry is something I could always do best,
And I always seem to put everything to a test.

Well this time I almost failed you see,
And the grade system did not go from A to E.

And on the line was me and you,
But passing is something I did do.

Our friendship, the one thing I could not do without,
I almost wrecked because of doubts.

I never meant to hurt you, or even make you mad,
I was just trying to understand why we were sad.

But I can't run and hide, not this time,
I had to say sorry so things could be fine.

I always let things sit too long on the shelf,
But now I have only to blame myself.

I am lucky you are understanding and such a good friend,
Something I will never doubt again.

I have always hurt people in the present and past,
But I can finally say I've learned at last.

That some things are better not seen or heard,
Because you can destroy the best with a couple of words.

And even though days will come when we may not say a thing at
all,
I will know it is not because of me, and that there is no need to
call.

That you would like to be by yourself, alone,
And should you want to talk, you would just pick up the phone.

So for what I have done I am sorry once more,
And I promise I will never again open that door.

THROUGH THE YEARS

I don't know how to say this, words just aren't enough,
How much your friendships valued, this one's a little tough.

When little fights come our way and things don't seem as clear,
And all of are happy thoughts turn into a pool of tears.
Or misunderstandings that we may have when the time comes.
I won't just leave without a word, and forget what you've done.
Your friendship I will not let go,
For you have helped me more than you know.
You took the time to listen and the time to care,
No matter what you somehow always let me know you're there.
I was never going to get close enough to anyone you see,
But you taught me how to trust again and accepted me for me.
You never once were cruel and you've never lied,
And when things got too much for me to handle inside.
I could always talk to you, tell you what was on my mind,
It's not only because you listened, you just simple took the time.
So when your turn comes around,
I promise I won't let you down.
I'll take the time, if you need a hand,
A listener, a friend, someone to understand.
Through arguments and laughter, through happiness and tears,
One thing you can count on our friendship through the years.
And should the road get rocky and the other at times sad,
I promise to stay your friend through the good times and the bad.
No one said becoming friends was easy and staying friends
harder yet,
That's when the rule comes in to forgive and forget.
But there's nothing I can think of that would make me want to end,
The fact that you are a very good friend.
So I'll tell you something that is as true as true can be,
You also Dave, mean the world to me.

Tracey Pizzino

AT THIS POINT

I don't know what I was thinking of, to believe what he said,
I can't figure out what was going through my head.

You have been nothing but nice to me,
And always spoke the truth from what I see.

Never once mean, that's not you,
Joking around a lot, but I did too.

I was going to just leave and not say good-bye,
But that's not me, I couldn't if I tried.

So to your house I went to explain how I felt,
I had to make a choice from the cards dealt.

I was so mad, and I guess I still maybe,
But he was calling a bluff, which he didn't think I'd see.

Well I hope he has learned, lies get people nowhere, no way, no how,
And friends with him I never was, not then, not now.

I know you would have found out sooner or later his plan,
I just hope you know why I did what I did and understand.

I place a lot of value on friendships, good or bad,
And I'll stick with it till the end should one make me sad.

But a lie I will not deal with, in any shape, form or way,
And I refuse to make an exception of that rule today.

I hope you really know how much your friendship means,
Because a friend like you is few and very far between.

I can talk to you about whatever is on my mind,
You are always willing to listen and seem to have the time.

So to someone I have met only a few months ago,
Your friendship is one thing I won't let go.

And I hope our friendship will always stay,
As strong as it is at this point today.

FRIENDS II

I would like to explain the best I can,
And that is with paper and pen in hand.
Things started out just as fine as can be,
Then we were friends you and me.
Then I started calling you everyday,
And we always managed to find something to say.
Then I said some things which now I regret,
Because I shouldn't have gotten mad, I just wanted to forget.
When I stopped by after work you had a hard day,
And you were trying to sleep, but it didn't matter anyway.
Because I left that day and felt hurt too,
Then I started crying because of you.
I wish I never would have found out,
But that was something I could do nothing about.
Then days pass on like they always do,
And things were different with me and you.

Things were the opposite just a few hours before,

Then that night you slammed in my face the door.

I am sure you didn't know it at the time,

Because the door only slammed in my mind.

And if that big talk would have taken place,

Again tears would fall down my face.

Yes, I will admit I did something wrong,

But you don't have to worry about me, I am strong.

I will handle things that come my way,

Even if they turn my sky grey.

I was being honest and serious with you,

A part time friend no can do.

If you wish I shall give you the space all friends need,

But I shall always be here for you in deed.

There were times I will say,

When I did want to call you on a certain day.

Just to see if you were alright,

But then I just put the phone down and turned off the light.

I don't want to risk the friendship at hand,

So could you please tell me just where it stands?

I'd go through hell, if that's what it has come to,

To find the answer that is true.

No matter how much it would hurt in the end,

The truth is all I ask for again.

The question is simple, before I go,

Are we still friends, YES or NO.

I'LL HOLD ON TO OUR FRIENDSHIP

The first day I met you was out on the lot,

And what you said I have not forgot.

Do you remember what you said?

Or is that day gone from your head.

Well just in case I'll tell you,

If you don't believe me, oh well it's true.

I was walking to my car and stopped to help you out,

Then I turned to leave and you said I'm Mickey if you have a doubt.

I got in my car a little puzzled at that time,

I wondered what was going through your mind.

Then things were okay again,

I said hi to you every now and then.

That day in the cafeteria was the next thing to be.

I was sitting next to Rick with you across from me.

He said some things and you sat there and laughed along,

Yet you didn't think you were in the wrong.

I gave you dirty looks for three days straight,

Assume was all you did, that you I did hate.

Then I called Dave and at his house you were,

At first you didn't know me things were a blur.

Then you figured out who I was, you were no longer in a lurch,

But yet you didn't stop to think about what was said, did it hurt.

Then days passed by as they always do,

And I became friends with you.

There are some things that piss me off, you already know,

But remember I'll try anything before I let go.

Of a friendship that means a lot to me, the good and bad I'll take,

The only thing I will not allow is a friend who is fake.

Just be yourself that's good enough for me,

And my bad side, pray you never have to see.

Never lie, no matter how much hurt may form,

Tracey Pizzino

Because friendships are fragile and easily torn.
Never make promises you don't intend to keep,
And never be afraid if the time comes to weep.
Never try to cross a person, whom you consider a friend,
Because it all comes back to you in the end.
I may not have known you long,
But as our friendship it is strong.
And growing with each passing day,
We always have something to say.
And sooner or later a fight we'll get in,
But it won't matter who will lose or win.
Just as long as we remain friends,
And don't let little things make it end.
I promise you I won't let you down,
I'll try my best to never see you frown.
If you ever need a listener, a shoulder or advice,
I hope you know I'm there for you, don't even think twice.
I'll never say things that you only wish to hear,
I will always be truthful and very sincere.
But above all else I'll be your friend forever,
No matter how long, this just remember.
You shall always have a special place in my heart and mind,
Because friends like you are rare to find.
Well there you have it; I see our friendship to be true,
I wonder if it looks that way to you.
There's one more thing before I go,
Something I hope you already know.
I'll hold on tight to our friendship, this to you I claim,
And when times are good or bad I pray you do the same.

AS YOU GO AWAY

This is going to be a little sad,

About the good times and some bad.

When I was down, you'd be there,

Always telling me that you cared.

To try and make me happy again,

You always considered me as a friend.

When I was sick or felt down,

You would always be around.

You listened to my problems everyday,

And yet you never had anything bad to say.

You never lied no matter how bad the truth would be,

You helped me open my eyes and see.

The mistakes I was making in my life,

You helped me through the pain and strife.

I just hope I was always there for you,

And your problems I helped you through.

I know I have told you this before,

You are not just a friend, but more.

One of my best friends that is you,

You helped some of my dark skies turn blue.

Well again I am sad today,

For I have found out you are going away.

Please don't misunderstand; I am happy for you,

And I hope you succeed in whatever you do.

But a good friend I will have to let go,

A friend who has helped me more than he knows.

I shall remember till the end,

And always think of you as my good friend.

And pray you are safe and glad,

And hope you never get sad.
But I have some questions, only a few,
That only consists of us two.
I was wondering if our friendship will last,
I know it can't be like the past.
I won't talk to or see you twice a week,
But yet the memories I shall keep.
But in the back of my mind,
Is the question, will it last through time?
Will our friendship continue to grow?
Or melt away like the snow.
I don't know the answers or what they might be,
I just know what this friendship means to me.
But in my mind you shall always stay,
No matter how far you go away.
But a few more things before I say good-bye,
I can't promise I won't cry.
One last thing that is true,
When you leave I will miss you.

IS THE COST TO HIGH

I'll try to explain best I can,
And that is with pen in hand.
Understand, I really can't say,
So let's go about it another way.
I told you there would be no lies at all,
No matter how far I might fall.
So I'm not going to start now,
I'll find a way to tell you somehow.

What happened on the lot was stupid you see,

It only had to do with me.

I brought it all on myself, that I won't deny,

But still I didn't want you to find out, that I went out there to cry.

I did not want to make you fell bad,

Because of the fact I was sad.

I would have been fine later on that night,

But yet that still doesn't make it right.

At first I did it to see what you'd do,

Then I started thinking it through.

The possibility of me getting in the way,

Of the two of you on any day.

Was it going to be like before?

To have found a good friend and have them shut the door.

That's when all hell broke lose, the only thing left for me,

Was to pretend I didn't care what was to be.

But for me to put myself in the position whether now or then,

I promised myself never would I be a part time friend.

Will it be the same, or is the cost to high,

And if that day comes and goes will I have to say good-bye.

I said something once that I can relate to you,

It's a hard decision to make, but it's one I must do.

I will be the one, who has to role the dice,

And I shall be the one to pay the price.

But will it be worth the cost,

To gamble our friendship then to have lost.

We are good friends and that is how it shall stay,

And it will last forever an a day.

I hope you understand a little better now,

I had to find answers out somehow.

I had to push it to the line,

To see if things would work out fine.

And should the day come, I'll do my best,

And pray I do things right to pass the test.

But until that day I promise to be,

The best kind of friend to you that you have been to me.

I REFUSE TO SHED A TEAR

This friendship was strange and full of pain,

Nothing to lose, yet nothing to gain.

I thought things were great and fine,

Then things came to the surface with time.

I'll try to summarize the best I see,

From the start when you became friends with me.

We worked together, you seemed kind,

Then we became friends in time.

You would come up to work a lot,

Remember those days, no, you probably forgot.

I found out later you had a girlfriend all along,

And things between you both were strong.

I had no problem with that you see,

Because you were only a friend to me.

We started calling each other too,

I would come over your house to talk to you.

Many hours would come and go,

We mostly talked of your girlfriend though.

From what you would tell me she seemed real nice,

Yet I never knew being your friend was such a high price.

You loved her and she loved you,

Any moron could tell that was true.

I wanted to meet her someday, somehow,

She won't understand, you said not now.

She would get mad for you having a friend,

Because I was a girl was how it did end.

Nothing more was said, then I asked you to tell Kristen of me,

You said no our friendship she won't let be.

I still didn't understand until one day,

I told you to tell her, what could she say.

I didn't see the big deal of being your friend,

And you told me there and then.

She knows we are friends and hates it too,

She said some things and I said good-bye to you.

I didn't want to cause trouble no matter what was lost,

I wasn't going to be friends with you, having you two the cost.

I told you that more than one time,

Things were hard, and then things were fine.

Then you came up to work after a month and a half had gone by,

You guys had broken up, I didn't know why.

She still hated me, your friends would say,

But there was nothing I could do, no way.

Well friends again we became,

There was still confusion and some pain.

Then it happened your nightmare came true,

I came over and on the phone talked about you.

To Kristen the person who did not like me one bit,

She didn't yell, or bitch, or try to hit.

I went over to her house for a chat that was long over due,

We both found out some shit about you.

You lied to both of us, and I wonder why,

You did everything in your power to protect your hide.

You wanted her to think we were more than just friends,

And you didn't care who you hurt in the end.

That's where you made your first mistake,

And in our hands you left your fate.

Well I hate to disappoint you, but things turned out right,

I left with Kristen being my friend that night.

She is no longer mad and doesn't blame me,

We are placing the blame on thee.

You guessed it on the very first try,

So could you please make us understand why?

Before it was hard to let go,

But this time no sadness will even show.

Before I forgave you and on with my life I did live,

But our friendship is over, because this I can't forgive.

I don't know if you care, but either way,

Tomorrow I shall start a brand new day.

If you have learned than that's fine,

If not then I was wasting my time.

I use to worry about you, if you were safe,

But now I don't want to remember your face.

I wonder if anything you said was true,

But I could never believe again what was said by you.

Do whatever you want; you won't hear a word from me,

And if you die, it's how you wanted it to be.

But I'll promise you one thing, I won't cry,

Because I refuse to shed a tear for a friend that did lie.

A FRIEND IN ME

I know you're hurt and blue,

And there is really nothing I can do.

I can try to help out if need be,
By listening like you have done for me.
And as a friend I shall always be there,
To give advise or just be a friend to let you know I care.
You have helped me out more than you know,
And taught me that no matter how hard it is best to let go.
Well now it is your turn to need a sincere friend,
And I shall be there till the end.
But like I told someone before,
It's best to be ready for what's in store.
That I am the one, who rolled the dice,
So I was the one to pay the price.
To hope it was worth the cost,
To gamble a friendship, then to have lost.
That is one fault which has proven true,
I have always valued the friends which I knew.
A little too much some people would say,
But that is how I live everyday.
I hope my being friends with you is good and not bad,
Because I already made one person sad.
And that is one thing I would not like to do,
But I just hope my helping does not hurt you.
But I have babbled on enough you see,
I am trying to prepare you for what might be.
But before I go there are two more things,
If you ever need to talk just give me a ring.
And remember no matter how things might be,
You shall always have a friend in me.

Tracey Pizzino

ONLY FOR YOURSELF

It doesn't matter where you are,
It doesn't matter where you go.
It doesn't matter what you do,
It doesn't matter who you know.

It shouldn't matter to anyone,
It shouldn't matter what they see.
It shouldn't matter either way,
It shouldn't matter what could be.

It only matters to yourself,
It only matters to a friend.
It only matters in your eyes,
It only matters in the end.

Just be the person you wish for,
Just try your best to make it come true.
Just make the effort everyday,
And the only person surprised will be you.

For if you try your hardest,
For you and only you.
Then you won't have to hide,
Cause there is nothing you can't do.

So when you start to doubt the things,
You have worked so hard to get.
Take a deep breath and remember,
The past that others forget.

That you were good at the start,
But now there's something more.
You are still a good person,
Just better than before.

And when the time comes when you see,
The change, and can be proud or yourself too.
That's when people who are your friends,
Shall have the chance to love you.

No more walls, will be put up,
To stop the people who have cared all a long.
And no more will you be hurt,
All the time, but twice as strong.

So when the day comes,
You'll know somehow.
And I'm happy to say,
That day is now.

I'VE ALWAYS TRIED TOO HARD

I've always tried to answer things,
Which were better left undone.
I've always tried to figure out,
Who lost or won.

I've always tried to see things,
That others couldn't see.
I've always tried to make things,
The best they could be.

I've always tried to make my friends,
Understand the wrong and right.
I've always tried to find the reason,
Why I cry at night.

I've always tried to hard,
Some would always say.
I've always tried to help people,
Go their own way.

But now my trying is over,
And others must learn too.
That sometimes always trying,
Is the wrong thing to do.

Some things you must accept,
Or in silence stay.
You have lived your life,
So let them live their way.

And some may take a wrong turn,
But who, we shall never tell.
All we can do in silence,
Is watch them go through hell.

It may take awhile,
And for some it maybe to late.
But no matter what they have chosen,
We could never hate.

But that's where it stops,
And we put back in their hands.
The life they will live,
And pray they understand.

But hope is all we can do,
And pray to the end.
That they'll see the wrong,
And get help my friend.

I WONDER HOW

I wonder how things will be,
When you have left and there's only me.
I wonder how it will go,
Will I always worry about a friend I know.
I wonder how I shall feel,
Toward the friendship that was so real.
Will I be able to at any moment recall?
The good and bad times, with us all.
We had great times and talks too,
But what should I say when my friend goes through.
With this plan to better himself,
Should I put my feelings on a shelf?
Or would it be better to tell him straight,
That his decision I really hate.
Don't get me wrong, I am happy for what he's going to be,
But when he leaves will he forget me.
I have lost friends, present and past,
Some friendships were good, and just didn't last.

But to lose his friendship, would hurt a lot more,

We did have our fights, and break down a door.

But I have known him my whole life through,

And in case you haven't guessed this is for you.

When the day comes when I need advice on a little thing,

How will I talk to you my phone won't ring.

You will not be anywhere near,

And all I can do is think my dear.

And wonder at any given point of a day,

Now think, what would Ricky say.

Would you tell me I took the right action?

Would you say its satisfaction?

Or would you just laugh and say,

As usual you took the wrong way.

I know it will be awhile before I hear from you,

Because writing is one thing you hate to do.

But letters from me you shall get,

To remind you that I did not forget.

About my friend who had a goal, a plan,

And reached for it with both hands.

Because whether I knew it then or now,

You did the right thing somehow.

But fours years is a long time too,

And I can't help but wonder will our friendship make it through.

The time for which you are gone,

I pray and hope I am wrong.

That this is only a test,

And our friendship is the best.

And always right here will I be,

Just like you have been for me.

But I shall wonder for days on end,

If you are safe and happy friend.
But my fears will ease at only one time and place,
And that is when I can see your face.
That's when I'll know you are alright,
And that's the day I'll sleep at night.

THINGS TO SAY BEFORE YOU GO

There are some things to say before you go,
Most of them you already know.
But just to keep them fresh in your mind,
And to let you know that you can always find.
A friend whenever you need one near by,
And one that shall always try.
To help out whenever need be,
I'll always be around to help, you'll see.
To never in a million years let you down,
To always seem to care if you are wearing a frown.
To think of you each passing day,
To always somehow find a way.
To help out if in a tight spot,
To remember the good days which I haven't forgot.
To remember the times you stood by me,
When everything was bad, you I would see.
Right there for me to talk to,
To have someone listen till I was through.
You gave me advice when I never once said too,
But through it all you were true.
A true blue friend, with something good to say,
No matter how bad things were that day.

Tracey Pizzino

You told me I was strong for what I'd been through,
But most of my strength came from you.
You wouldn't let me give in, you wouldn't hear of it,
No matter what was done you knew I wouldn't quit.
So now as I have relived the past,
I'll tell you what I wish to say at last.
For you have choose to up and go,
To only better a person I know.
To work towards a future big and bright,
To do something you feel is right.
I am proud of what you will do,
And I am positive you'll make it through.
With flying colors and most of all,
I know you won't quit if you should fall.

But for me this will be hard,
Again I'll have to put up my guard.
It won't be easy to say good-bye,
But I'll try my hardest not to cry.
But should the day come when a little voice you hear,
It's me to let you know I'm here.
And that you are anything but alone,
No matter how far you are from home.
I'll say a little prayer at each days end,
To help protect a special friend.
And just so you know what I'll say,
I'll be glad to write it in this poem today.
     If you are listening above,
     Please look after a friend I love.
     He has always been there for me,
     I can't let him down, I hope you see.

For he has decided to go away,

Just keep an eye on him everyday.

And try to remind him if you will,

That when a wind comes and gives him a chill.

I am thinking of him again,

And I'll be there until the end.

I'll never ever let him go,

For he is the best friend I shall ever know.

Again thank you for all you have done,

Because with you by him, he has already won.

Well that is my prayer, which I shall say,

At the end of each passing day.

Please stay safe and take care my friend,

Until the day we meet again.

But one thing please remember,

Friends we shall stay forever.

And with each day that I pass through,

Will be another day I'll miss you.

MY FINAL GOOD-BYE

I really don't know what to do or say,

I found out a couple things today.

I won't try to say I don't miss you,

Because that is a fact that is so true.

But as much as I miss our friendship dear,

You are the last person I wish to be near.

Maybe you speak before you know what you say,

But I can't believe you are acting this way.

You are being so cruel and mean,

And all the things that come between.

You are talking about your friends like they are nothing you see,

I can't help but wonder the things you say about me.

You always told me you would never say anything bad about anyone,

But there is a big difference between what you've said and done.

I thought the day I saw you would make me oh so sad,

But to tell you the truth I didn't feel bad.

A little sick that you were such a good friend,

But I can live with my decisions in the end.

I wanted to be your friend, just give it one more chance,

But at this moment and time, your way I don't even want to glance.

You have changed a lot, but that is up to you,

I am no one to tell you what to do.

I don't want to see you hurt, but that's as far as it will go,

Your friendship meant a lot to me, but now, I just don't know.

Maybe us not being friends is really for the best,

So I can have time to think and take a rest.

If I am being a bitch, I apologize,

I am just beginning to open my eyes.

You have a problem, for which you can't see,

You take everything as a joke and not reality.

You hide behind walls that are only around you,

That you are always right, and there's only one side not two.

You were a good friend, and most likely still could be,

But for now, you are better off without me.

Or maybe I am much better off too,

That I am no where near you.

I shall always wonder how you are doing, if all is good and well,

And I shall always miss you, some can always tell.

But going separate ways, just had to be done,

I wasn't glad to do it, and it was no fun.

But for some reason I am happy now,

And I hope down the line you get help somehow.

Good-bye Ryan, for we won't meet again,

But I am glad I had the chance to become your friend.

ANOTHER DAY TO THINK OF YOU

I don't know why I thought of you today,

But my mind just went that way.

For some reason I saw you,

Imagination, yes, but it seemed true,

It has been five days now,

And everyday I think of you somehow.

Something someplace, when I look and see,

I think of the friendship between you and me.

I hope you think and know I care,

But it's better if I'm not there.

I really can't say how I feel at all,

The only way would be to ask and call.

But that is one thing I must not do,

I can't give in and call you.

I don't know why this is so hard,

It was me, who put up the guard.

Remember that question I asked of you,

The one you could not understand that day too.

Well maybe now you can comply,

To the purpose I asked and know why.

Is it better to protect yourself, or stay friends?

Even if you, yourself will be hurt in the end.

Well I made my choice that one day,

But now I should have gone the other way.

Because the hurt may not have been so bad,

Or thoughts of a friend make me sad.

But my decision was made back then,

And all I can do is remember when.

I thought I had done the right thing,

By saying everything, holding no strings.

But I am the one, who rolled the dice,

So I must pay the price.

I just hope it was worth the cost,

To gamble a friendship, then to have lost.

I don't even know how you think of this to be,

Do you think of the friend you lost, me.

Maybe this does not even faze you,

It happened, it's over, now move on through.

I just hope this pain I put upon myself,

Was for something and not put on a shelf.

Because it would hurt more, if you didn't care,

And I was just a fill in friend when the others weren't there.

But I can't believe that to be true,

I must believe I was a friend to you.

But now it is time for me to go,

And I just wish I could know.

Do you miss our talks like me?

Do you take the time to see?

If you could figure out what went wrong,

Or was our friendship just not that strong.

That maybe we are still friends,

Just talking now and then.

Whatever the answers to this maybe,

Only we have the key.

And only know our own solution,

Whether it is good or pollution.

But good or bad no one knows,

But it is time for me to go.

But remember one thing that is true,

Another day will come when I think you.

But until that day, I shall pray for again,

The person I said good-bye to, a good friend.

DECEMBER 19, 1989

I wondered how the day would end,

When I finally saw you again.

But I saw your mother first, and yet,

There was not one thing I did regret.

She asked me why I was not talking to you,

As though it was old or new.

But it is still the same old plan,

But this time I can't understand.

I have called you and come over a lot,

Never bringing up the pain, I choose to forgot.

I even understood you not wishing me a happy birthday,

For you were getting things ready for the baby on the way.

But now it is December 19, 1989,

And you still haven't found the time.

To call and tell me you had a bundle of joy,

And it was a girl and not a boy.

I am going to wait and see,

Just how long before you call me.

Not a moment goes by when I don't think of you,

But there is nothing more I can do.

All I know is I did try,

To communicate and talk, but now I cry.

You couldn't just call me up and say,

You were fine and had a girl the other day.

I wanted to be there, on that day so bad,

When I found out I was only sad.

It seems now that you didn't want me around,

So I had to stand my ground.

I wish I knew just where we stand,

But like I said before I just don't understand.

I thought we were getting along great again,

But I guess that was my first mistake friend.

Best friends I don't know if we'll ever be,

Right now just friends are a little hard to see.

But the date of Dec. 2, 1989 will be with me till the end,

It's the day you said good-bye my friend.

That day your life was full you see,

Now there is no need for me.

Please always stay safe and take care,

And remember if you had called, I'd of been there.

HURT IS NOT THE WORD

If you think it didn't hurt, then you were wrong,

If you think it didn't hurt, and that I'm strong.

If you think it didn't hurt, what I had to do,

If you think it didn't hurt, when I said good-bye to you.

If you think it didn't hurt, then you don't know me,
If you think it didn't hurt, well, you'll never know or see.

Cause if you think it didn't hurt, then maybe it was you,
That you're the one that didn't care when the out come, came through.

Because I knew it hurt, and you were wrong,
I knew it hurt, and that I'm not strong.

I knew it hurt, when I said good-bye to you,
I knew it hurt, but it's something I had to do.

Yes, I knew it hurt, more than you could see,
And I knew it would hurt, but it was for you, none of it for me.

I'll try to keep my mind on the way I choose it to end,
That it was my decision to say good-bye my friend.

But if you call there is nothing I could do,
Except try my hardest not to call you.

It is for the best, I must say,
And now I must go day by day.

So again good-bye to you, from me,
And maybe the hurt you can see.

But I did do it for not one selfish thing,
With no comments and no strings.

Maybe in time you can forget it all,
And have the decency not to call.

Because every time you do, it opens the door,
And it gets that much harder to close once more.

Just take care and be happy friend,
And maybe one day we shall meet again.

And until that time I can only try,
To believe I did the right thing by saying good-bye.

TO YOU I SAY GOOD-BYE

I wonder if you even know,
How much it hurt, when I let go.

To our friendship, good and true,
It wasn't for me, I did it for you.

Your happiness is more important, you see,
No matter what the consequences would be to me.

I did not want to make you two fight at all,
That's why I told you not to call.

I had to break free with no strings,
And yet still remember things.

Like the talks we use to have a lot,
And some bad which I forgot.

But now reality, the bad has become,
Yet not one person has really won.

Both of you put me right between you two,
There was nothing more I could do.

Accept try to make you see at last,
We must live now, not in the past.

I hope you two are happy one day again,
And always recall me as a good friend.

But this is my way to help out,
So Kristen won't be mad or have doubts.

Just know in my mind a friend you shall stay,
And no one will ever take that away.

You were a great friend I shall always remember,
And as a friend I shall miss you forever.

Because friends like you are important to me,
Even if I had to let go and set you free.

And that is what I had to do,
And it hurt a lot when I said good-bye to you.

Tracey Pizzino

JUST US THREE

How do you think things would be?
If it was just you, him and me.

The sky would always be blue and clear,
No lies, or heartaches and not one tear.

We would all get along with no fights, not one,
We would never have to be mad by what was said or done.

Everything would be perfect, not one fault at all,
No one would get hurt, no one would fall.

It sounds like a fantasy land,
All of us together and it would be grand.

But I think I will take the friendship we had,
Even though at times we made each other mad.

We still care about the other one,
Even after things were said and done.

We accepted the pain of the past as well as the happiness,
We had good times, bad times and some bliss.

But together as friends through it all we stayed,
Though at times we thought each other strayed.

Yet we are all still friends,
And it is far from the end.

We had some good times walking down memory lane,
Thinking of all the remember when's and all the pain.

But I promise that through good and bad,
I will stand by when one is sad.

To try my best to understand,
To always lend a helping hand.

And above the rest always remember,
We can do anything with the three of us together.

And if I ever get a chance to wish for one thing,
It would not be for money or the power of a king.

But instead I shall wish for one thing to always be,
And that is friends forever, just us three.

SAY GOOD-BYE TO YOU

I really don't know how to feel at all,
One minute you're not talking then you say to call.

The longer we're friends the less we have to say,
I am deeply regretting a new day.

For tomorrow will be here to soon for me,
I don't know if we'll stay friends, if it should be.

Tracey Pizzino

I don't want to cause trouble for you,
That is the last thing I would do.

I write you letters on how I see things to be,
And not once do you tell me.

How you feel about anything anymore,
It's like you got up and shut the door.

Don't you feel that I will help out?
Or is our friendship giving you doubts.

If that is the case I think we both know,
It is time for us to go.

Our separate ways and say good-bye,
So we won't have to think about the "what ifs" and "why".

It seems as though me you can no longer trust,
And in a friendship that is a must.

Maybe you were just having a bad day,
And there is no truth to a word I might say.

But I will only know your side if you care to share,
And I'm hoping it's enough for you to know I'm always there.

But if it's not and this is the end,
Take care of yourself and be happy my friend.

And you I shall never forget,
Or regret the day we met.

A good friend to me you always seemed,
We did have fights but did dream.

Always recall the good times if you will,
But when those memories start to give you a chill.

Then it's time to forget the bad as well as the good too,
And when that day comes I'll say good-bye to you.

YOUR FRIEND

I tired to be friends, and it was going good,
Nothing going on, nothing ever would.

Then you showed me letters that your girlfriend wrote,
Not just one, but a couple of notes.

But I remained calm, and showed not one tear,
Trying so hard to hide the hurt and fear.

Then we talked like the best of friends,
And it was like that till the nights end.

Then I didn't talk to you for a day or two,
For you were grounded for what you do.

Then you called me to see if I was mad,

But at the same time you sounded sad.

That's when you told me, you broke up with her,
My brain didn't work, things were a blur.

I kept asking you questions and you couldn't understand why,
I was doing my best to help or at least try.

But I told you, the two of you would be back together,
I did say that or don't you remember.

Then after work you wanted me to stop by,
We talked just a little, and then said bye.

I am doing a lot better, but every now and then,
It is still kind of hard to be your friend.

I'LL ALWAYS BE HERE

I told you I'd be there if you ever need a hand,
A shoulder to cry on or someone to understand.

I'll try to be strong when you are down,
I'll try to make you smile instead of frown.

I'll try not to lecture you as much as before,
I'll always be prepared for what's in store.

I'll never say good-bye without a good fight,
I'll never let your bright days turn to night.

But after all is said and done,
I'm not here to say I won.

I had to somehow make you see,
Just how much it did hurt me.

And that is why I bitch a lot,
And was pissed when you forgot.

But I hope you understand now,
That I had to help somehow.

Whether it is night or day,
I'll always somehow find a way.

It may be in person or by phone,
Either at work or at home.

But one thing please always know,
Come hell, high water or eight feet of snow.

I shall always be a friend to you,
No matter what other people say or do.

And our friendship I will always recall,
To be the best of all.

And should the time come to shed a tear,
Just please remember I'll always be here.

And I hope our friendship continues to grow,
Because how much it means to me, you'll never know.

LEAVING AGAIN

Hello, and how are you today,
I hope happy and not gray.

It was good to have you home,
Though I only saw you a couple times though.

It was as if you had never been gone,
Everything was good, everyone strong.

Only thinking of the present day,
And regretting when you would go away.

Trying to make the most each time,
Not showing the sadness in our minds.

Then that day it came to fast,
But now we have to remember the past.

You had to go back this afternoon,
If you ask me it was too soon.

But that is something you wanted to do,
And I am with you through and through.

Six months may seem too long,
But I can handle it and stay strong.

Just because you are no longer around,
Doesn't mean I should be down.

I can still write you a letter or two,
And it would be the same as talking to you.

Of course I won't get a fast reply,
But there is no need for me to cry.

A friend is a friend, a person full of grace,
And no one could ever take one's place.

I do miss you, but then again,
I should be happy you are my friend.

One more thing before I depart,
Something only from the heart.

Please, stay safe and take care,
And if you need a friend, I'll be there.

A FRIEND SO TRUE

A friend is someone you will always know,
A friend forever no matter where they go.

Tracey Pizzino

Always there should you need a hand,
Someone to listen and understand.

Boy or girl, it should make no difference at all,
Because both will be there if you should fall.

What I did to deserve your friendship, one can only guess,
But one thing is for certain, with it I was blessed.

And that is one thing that I hope will always be,
The friendship between you and me.

This is the way I see you,
A friend forever and always true.

I know you won't lie, no matter how bad the truth maybe,
No matter what, that I can easily see.

So with that in mind and above the rest,
You my friend deserve the best.

So for now good-bye until we meet again,
And through heaven or hell you shall stay my friend.

So now you know what my definition of a friendship is, so true,
And with honors I say this applies to you.

So no matter if we should go our separate ways,
And just think back to the yesterdays.

You are a friend I will never ever forget,
And becoming your friend I will never regret.

But I just hope one day I can be,
As good of a friend to you, as you have been to me.

WE MISS YOU

When we **first started** we couldn't see,
We didn't **know how** things would be.

Could we **blend in**, plain as day?
Or will people just walk away.

Then came the day we met so blue,
And none of our nightmares did come true.

You see I finally got to know you at a party one night,
When I tired to tell you wrong from right.

I have already apologized before,
But I would like to say sorry once more.

But you were nice and kind from the beginning,
We needed no act to come out winning.

And winning is something we did do,
And to show for it we have a great friend, you.

You accepted us for who we were, nothing more or less,
And as a result with your friendship we were blessed.

You have treated us as equals since the first day,
That is more than others can say.

You told us we could come to you should a problem form,
Anything from a sunny day to a terrible storm.

No matter how good or how bad,
You want us to smile not stay sad.

So please remember and always know,
No matter where it is you go.

A friend to us you shall always be,
A friend to her, a friend to me.

So when the day comes to say we miss you,
Bet on anything that it's true.

SO SORRY

I was not going to write you another letter or poem you see,
I was not even going to talk to you, if that could be.

I was going to let it go as a friend that went away,
But I have only met you four weeks ago today.

I had no right writing you or asking you to call,
I am just trying to forget it all.

Me and you are very much the same,
We try to help other people no matter who's to blame.

If they walk on us we forgive and sooner or later forget,
I will always remember and never regret the day we met.

You were so nice to me, all the time,
Good friends I have learned are hard to find.

But I have found someone very nice, you,
I know for a fact that is true.

If I bugged you at all in anyway,
I would like to apologize today.

For anything I may have said or done,
Like at the party, your day for fun.

I should have kept my nose out of where it didn't belong,
Because all I did and said was wrong.

I don't know you good enough to try and tell you how I felt,
About the way you walked away and how the problem was dealt.

So please forgive me for budding in where I should not have been,
And I hope we can remain friends.

I won't ask you to write, or talk to me everyday,
Just when you are gone, sometimes remember me okay.

Good-bye for now and good luck too,
Take care of yourself and all you do.

I will miss your happy face,
But none of my friends take another ones place.

THE NICEST ONE

I really don't know you, I must say,
Though I have only worked with you a couple of days.

And those days I will recall,
Were some of the best days of all?

You were friendly and kind too,
You would tell jokes when I'd bag for you.

Then one day out of the blue, by surprised, me you did take,
So seriously you asked me if I ate cookie dough not baked.

My answer was yes, and you looked at me,
And said we have something in common I see.

Then you said you only have until August 5th to go,
For your last day of work, then a week before you go.

Into the service for your future plans,
If I clearly did understand.

But you will be missed, along with your happy face and personality too,
Because of all the people I met, the nicest one was you.

NOT THE GREATEST OF FRIENDS

I may not have been the greatest friend around,
And never once stood my ground.

You said I was stupid, among other things too,
But there were good times which I knew.

I don't know if you recall, or even care to remember,
But I know those days so well, all of us together.

Talking about things that had no meaning at all,
Always being around if someone would fall.

Causing trouble, but having fun,
Mostly on days full of sun.

Then one day it all fell apart and everyone went their own way,
Some of us stayed together, others went a stray.

I know I have told you this before,
But I don't think it will hurt to tell you once more.

We were never the closest of friends before you went away,
But for some reason I had to be there, and without a word to say.

At first I thought it was just to do you in,
That I couldn't let you have left and let you think you did win.

But then I finally understood why I did it now,
I had to say good-bye to you and patch things up somehow.

All the little fights, were just that, little,
But we let them build up and get in the middle.

And I never thought I would miss you not being home at last,
Even though things weren't that great in the past.

But I do miss you not being here,
Even though we did not talk for almost a year.

But that was one thing that you reminded me of a lot,
That no matter how mean people were to me, I always forgave
and forgot.

DIFFERENCES THAT NEVER CAME

I hope things could be different then they have in the past,
Like when the time comes when we say we don't care at last.

Because what we say and do are two different cases,
Cause we always think and see all the same faces.

That once caused us heartache and pain,
And some that kept us happy and sane.

We still wonder if a day will come to show,
The time for us to finally let go.

But to run and hide would not be right,
We could run day and night.

But something somewhere will always make us see,
And remind us of things that use to be.

So all we can really do until the end,
Is live one day at a time my friend?

LIVE IN TODAY

I wonder how the sky would seem,
If we could live forever in a dream.

Could we be happy every second of the day?
Or would we have to worry about getting hurt along the way.

Would it be peaceful, with flowers and the sun?
Would we just have 365 days of just fun?

Would there be waterfalls in every house around,
Would we always have a happy face instead of a frown?

Tracey Pizzino

Could we have a day to bring people in?
Could we change evil ways so we would win?

If we could live in a dream land with no faults at all,
Would we never have to pick each other up when we fall?

All of our friends would be the same,
They would never look at us to place the blame.

But yet I wonder in a perfect world could we have found,
Some of our friends who never let us down.

Sure they have a fault or two,
But they are always there for you.

I don't know if I could give it up for a dream,
All the imperfections are part of me.

All the fights, and the pain,
All the troubles and the gain.

We were taught how to be strong,
Even if the way they taught us was wrong.

So what I am really trying to say,
It is good to dream as long as we live in today.

TO ALL OF YOU

Before I turn to walk and go,
There are a few things you all should know.

There were some great times in which I will recall,
And I will always wear a smile when I think of you all.

I will never forget you no matter how far I may go,
You will always be a part of my heart and soul.

I will be sad when the day should appear,
But the friends I have made are so dear.

I will miss the laughter and pain,
Looking out the front window at the sun and the rain.

The bad days which weren't so bad?
And the days when I made some people sad.

You guys stood by me all the way,
And friends to me you all shall stay.

I would like to thank all of you, you see,
Because all of you accepted me for me.

So now I have to say good-bye to all of you once more,
Because I have the opportunity to open a new door.

Thank you all for the good times we had,
And please do not be sad.

I have learned a great deal from you,
And you always cheered me up when I was blue.

To Lisa, Donna, Millie etc... a friendly good-bye,
I hope you get all you're after in life and this is why.

Because you all are different then the rest,
And all of you here deserve the best.

SORRY IS IN ORDER

This is not to make you sad,
And this is not to make you mad.

This is to make you see at last,
The way I look at the present and past.

I used the past to run and hide,
When things were too much inside.

I blamed things on everyone else,
But never once blamed myself.

I also thought you were wrong,
And through it all I was strong.

But the strength I had, came from you,
By all the things you would say and do.

Some of them hurt and continued to cause some ache,
But you my friend I could not replace.

We have been through a lot of things we may never tell,
But we also had good times and also went through hell.

Sometimes I would wonder if you would ever call,
Then at the end of a day forget it all.

Because when the phone stopped ringing each day,
I knew we had nothing more to say.

And again blamed you for the frown I'd see,
When I looked in the mirror, but it was me.

Then things totally fell to the ground,
And again I thought you had let me down.

I had myself convinced you were gone forever,
And that I didn't want our friendship to return ever.

Then came today, the present again,
You showed up at my door, like we were always friends.

I wondered why you did it now,
And I had to find the answer somehow.

Then you started calling on the phone like you use to do,
And I knew something was wrong, it's too good to be true.

Tracey Pizzino

I didn't want to believe you or trust in you again,
I couldn't get my hopes up, that we were becoming friends.

I tried to back away, I tried to turn and run,
Because I just couldn't forget what was said and done.

Then finally you explained why, it's been so long,
And again I had to admit I was wrong.

You said you weren't using me, on that I could bet,
It's just going to take a lot of time for me to forget.

But I promise you one thing, which I plan to do,
Once again I will try to start believing in you.

However, I have some apologies in which I need to say,
Because it is mostly my fault things turned out this way.

Please don't argue and say everything is fine,
Because I have to say what's on my mind.

So for anything I said last night that offended you in any way,
I would like to apologize today.

I am sorry for the bad feelings and the way I yelled at you,
I am sorry for the smart remarks and being pissed too.

I am sorry for the rudeness, I am sorry for the lie,
I am sorry for not trusting you, for not giving you another try.

But most of all I am sorry for making you feel bad,
And I am really sorry for saying I wasn't mad.

I should have said what was bugging me,
That there was no way this could be.

But all that is over, done with through,
No more wishing for something knew.

I will take each day as it goes by,
And promise not to ever lie.

I won't jump to conclusions, if the facts aren't clear,
I will try to hold onto a friendship so dear.

I will also keep my nose out of where it don't belong,
And I will always admit my wrongs.

But also a thank you is in order you see,
Because through the good times and heartaches you stood by me.

We could always talk about things no matter what or who,
And I hope that we can continue to do,

I have learned a lot of stuff in the passed couple of days,
Some of them were good, but on some I'm not so crazed.

But I did answer my question and I will never doubt again,
The fact that me and you are very much friends.

Tracey Pizzino

WHY NOW

Things were fine from where I stood,
I was living again, for the good.

Yes, I thought about all the good times we shared,
And I always knew for you I'd care.

We were like brother and sister for 3 years now,
Then finally one day it fell apart somehow.

I was sad but learned to adjust,
For I didn't have anymore, a friend I could trust.

I saw at a distance what no one could see,
For they never knew the kind of friend you were to me.

I would wonder if you were safe,
But I never heard of anything being out of place.

The Christmas of '88' rolled through,
And again talking was me and you.

Then after New Year's things went down,
And again on my face was a frown.

But then time passed and I was fine,
I had everything straightened out in my mind.

I was finally getting on with my life you see,
I knew that was how it had to be.

I was already to try and forget the past,
I was getting on with my life at last.

Please don't get me wrong, I was glad to see you again,
And I want so much to believe we are really friends.

But could you please try to answer this somehow,
I just want to understand after all this time, Why Now?

TWO MONTHS LATER

The sky is clear, the air is dry,
I sit in my room and start to cry.

I think about the yesterdays and how it use to be,
Then I look at the now, a sad reality.

All the talks we use to have all the little fights,
All the wondering and hoping things turned out right.

All the little fun things we use to do,
Like seeing a movie and going shopping too.

But as time and school went by, then came graduation day,
That moment seemed to last forever than faded away.

You left for school and I was sad,
But you told me that it wouldn't be so bad.

Tracey Pizzino

Well then you said you were moving away with your family,
Then again I had to face reality.

But the whole time you never planned on leaving, you were staying right here,
Don't you know you put me through hell, or don't you even care?

I know you had things to do when you got back in town,
But I never thought in a million years you'd let our friendship down.

Well now it's been over two months since we had any talks,
Not a shopping trip, a movie not even a short walk.

It started out like no other, it was so strong,
I still can't figure out what went wrong.

Don't get me wrong I am not asking for your sighs,
I am not asking you to call me, I am not asking you to cry.

The only thing I ask of you is to think things through,
Think hard and carefully of what you're going to do.

Because when the time arrives for my phone to ring,
Tell me, what will you do if you hear not a thing.

I don't mean to hurt you or sound like a spoiled brat,
I would just like you to think about where we stand at.

Because the way I see things at this moment in time,
The friend I use to have, I can longer find.

I searched everywhere I even called her on the phone,
Then I finally I got her, she was home.

But she couldn't talk long, and called me back never,
But I am supposed to think our friendship is forever.

She did teach me a thing or two,
About what to and not to do.

She said the most important thing to do,
Is not to go to them have them come to you.

Well I waited and waited and still noting yet,
Then I thought maybe, NO she couldn't forget.

But stranger things happen in the world today,
And there is nothing more I can do or say.

Except I hope in the future I will meet again,
The person I lost, my best friend.

FRIEND IN ME

It's not to make you sad or down,
It's not to make you cry or frown.

It is a reminder that will always show,
That to me our friendship did grow.

It will sit there everyday and night,
To help you through wrongs and rights.

I will also just be there,
To let you know that I care.

And always as the birds fly free,
You will always have a friend in me.

But it will also remind you that till the end,
You are to me a true blue friend.

ALWAYS STAYED FRIENDS

Another year as we can see,
We always stayed friends you and me.

We just had little problems, but we cleared those up fast,
We just have a thing with people in our past.

They want to start trouble between me and you,
But as friends we managed to get through.

Sure we may not have talked everyday,
But always in our minds the other one stayed.

But please remember and always know,
That not one person could ever make me let go.

Of the friendship between you and me,
Because that is something that will always be.

It remained strong through the good and bad,
And it will be there if the other is mad.

But most important after all this time,
We can still talk about anything that's on our mind.

So happy birthday and have fun too,
And remember I will always stay a friend to you.

I hope you are happier than all the rest,
Because you my friend deserve the best.

I DON'T KNOW WHAT TO SAY

I don't know what to say or do,
I am very hurt and so confused.

This problem has been dwelling awhile,
And it makes me frown instead of smile.

My friends are my friends no matter color or sex,
But every time I turn around I have to defend them what the heck.

I am 18 and my life is still not my own,
Is he afraid to let me make decisions by myself, alone?

I lost his trust for no real reason you see,
Just because I have friends who are different then me.

He is holding on to tight and my life is going by,
I can't seem to make him understand why.

That I am happy with my friends you see,
And that is what they are going to stay, friends with me.

ME AND YOU BEST FRIENDS

How to act, what do I say?
Should I treat her in a different way?

Will she be hurt if I say why I'm mad?
Will she understand, I don't want to make her sad?

Or should I just forget it all, sit there and not even blink,
Than she'll never know exactly what I think.

That's how I see your answer to the first question,
Seeing how to handle me and then go in what direction.

Well the answer in my opinion is easier than it seems,
It's not something you have to make up or something that you
dream.

Just say what you feel, no matter the price,
Don't stop to think, is it mean or nice.

Don't underestimate me; I can accept the good, with the bad,
I can change if there' something I did to make you mad.

Or I could try to explain why I did it and take it from there,
Whether it was done on accident or because I care.

No matter what the reason, the answer should always be,
The truth when I'm talking to you or you to me.

The second question is tougher, but the meaning almost the
same,
For sometimes it's what was or wasn't said that begins the game.

Should I treat her different then I do the rest,
Will she understand that it's for the best?

Does she even realize how hard it is to change?
Something that was simple is now rearranged.

Before all my good friends were guys and that was all,
They could accept a punch and take a fall.

I could call them up and say hey, what's new,
And they'd say not much, how the hell are you.

But then the picture changed, along came me,
Things weren't has plain and simple as what was to be.

We became good friends, great ones if I may,
Then the trouble started, what do I say.

Can she take the fall like the rest always did?
But seriously who am I trying to kid.

You were scared to say things, afraid I'd break in two,
Never really saying if I offended you.

Always walking on shells like you didn't want to try,
To say something that would hurt me or make me cry.

Just treat me like the others if you're pissed off just say,
Try to understand, don't treat me a different way.

I will not fall to pieces should you say why you're mad,
I won't sit and wonder what I did that was so bad.

I'll be able to try and change it, so it doesn't happen again,
And at the same time know, you treat me equal, like a friend.

Maybe that's been the problem all along,
Not the issue who's right or wrong.

Not even that I made you mad enough, we'd stopped talking
again,
Not even to the point are we still friends.

Because you called everyone else, and never hardly me,
None of those are it, that now I see.

It was because of what I said before,
You had to get use to opening a different door.

Something you weren't use to, and maybe still have doubts,
But say if you were mad, friends work things out.

Even if it has nothing to do with me, I'll help in anyway,
No matter how mean the words are, you might say.

I'll always be here for you, like you have been for me,
That is one thing that will always be.

No matter what time of day, or what time at night,
For you I shall always have on a light.

And though it is hard for you to say what's on your mind,
Just know our friendship will last through time.

And nothing in the world will make our friendship lack,
For we have been to hell and back.

And though, through time, something's may get rearranged,
You Are My Friend Forever and That Will Never Change.

NEVER ALONE

When things go wrong, as they often do,
When you think everything is because of you.
When you sit and say the what ifs and why's,
When you want to run, but instead you cry.
Just know that everything happens for a reason, whether bad or good,
And you must know you always do what you should.

Tracey Pizzino

Things can't be perfect all the time,

Just like friends, you can't always find.

So when your days are filled with tears,

And nothing can take away your fears.

Count on your friends to help you through,

Because something's alone, you cannot do.

We may not be able to help, or change what was done,

But we are not going to let you go, by yourself as one.

I will always be right by your side should you ever need a friend,

A shoulder to cry on or advice to lend.

No matter how bad you see it right now,

I promise things will get better somehow.

I'll never walk away from you, and I'll always be right there,

Never too far away to let you know I care.

So to a brother I never had, I'd like you to know,

Come hell, high water, or eight feet of snow.

I'll do all I can to try and help you out,

Even when your mind is full of doubt.

So please let up, don't be so quick to judge the situation,

Because all that will cause you is aggravation.

Whether or not you feel like there is no one around,

And in the place of a smile is a permanent frown.

I know this won't make you feel any better, but I had to try,

Because I can't watch you roll over and die.

Just know and remember something that's true,

You are never alone, because we love you.

NOTHING'S WRONG

Nothing's wrong, everything is fine,

That seems to be your favorite line.

But it's plain to see by the look on your face,

Something's wrong, out of place.

Yet you try your best to say you're fine, there's nothing wrong,

And alone you try to handle it, because you are strong.

Well that doesn't work anymore,

Not like it did before.

You can say things are fine and grand,

Trying your hardest for me to believe and understand.

But that game is over, your secrets found,

The way you thought was so perfect and sound.

Your little phrase you use so often and well,

Explains the opposite of what you tell.

It's not that you're doing it on purpose you see,

It's a habit you are use to using so free.

So when the words are spoken and no one's around,

By yourself you can wonder and also frown.

But let a friend say are you alright,

Your defense kicks in, an over your head glows a light.

I'll try to help, just tell me what to do,

Because they always say one is not better than two.

So the next time you decide to walk around and pout,

And not let anyone know what it's all about.

And your answers the same time and time again,

For it's when "Nothing's Wrong" is said, is the time you most need a friend.

Whether you're happy or whether you're sad,

With all good things, there must be bad.

Yet that doesn't stop us from having fun,

From staying inside, when out is the sun.

Just try once in a while to let someone say,

Tell me what's wrong; I'll chase the blues away.

So when a friend walks up, have the courage and be strong,

And confide in that friend and say something's wrong.

A FRIENDSHIP CAKE

What to do if you are down,

Just be happy and don't frown.

Nothing is going to cheer you up, no matter what I say,

So I must go about this a different way.

I wish I could try to make you understand,

That this is nothing like we had planned.

To say you wish, you knew before, how it would be,

Is trying to look in the future and tomorrow see.

You must live day to day and handle whatever may come,

And when you get to an obstacle, fight until you've won.

But let's try and cheer you up, what could do the trick,

How about a cake that's really nice and thick.

It's a little something we are going to do,

Something that's old, yet something that's new.

We are going to cook a dish you see,
Of how things are to me.

First let's see what shall we bake,
Ah! Yes, a friendship cake.

You must first find a person with all the qualities you need,
Someone you can depend on indeed.

And once you have that, then the rest is a breeze,
We should make this cake with ease.

Now that we have all the ingredients to finish the recipe up,
Let's start by taking a level spoonful of patience, add it in a cup.

Then put a dash of knowledge an a sprinkle of care,
Then mix it up carefully then equally share.

Add some kindness an a cup of hearts,
Throw in politeness so it's not to tart.

Then combine with helpfulness and blend well,
Put in some ego so it can swell.

Then after that's done, add a last touch,
A tiny bit of happiness, but not too much.

Then add all ingredients to the most important of all,
Loyalty, to make sure the cake doesn't fall.

Add all the rest of your emotions and your personality traits,
Nothing could turn out better than something you just create.

No mess to clean, no dishes to do,
Nothing but pride will come through.

Hang up the apron, throw the towel down,
And put a smile in place of the frown.

For what you have made could have never been done,
By someone who quits, leaves and runs.

Only made and perfected by someone that who,
Have the qualities that make a best friend, like you.

Though faults are added, it doesn't compare,
To the good times and memories we have shared.

So when things are a little tough and you're far away,
Just know in my heart you shall always stay.

And look back at the recipe and read the words again,
Because it takes someone special to be a best friend.

JUST REMEMBER FOREVER

Just remember forever I will be fine,
Just remember forever you are in my mind.

Just remember forever through thick and thin,
Just remember forever it doesn't matter if we win.

Just remember forever all the good days,
Just remember forever all the good rays.

Just remember forever the fun times too,
Just remember forever me and you.

Just remember forever all the talks and sorrows,
Just remember forever today and tomorrow.

Just remember forever I will be there again and again,
Just remember forever you are my friend.

THIS IS THE DAY

This is the day I never wanted to be,
The day we had to separate you and me.

Since you are going away and I am staying here,
Just know and remember I will always care.

Looking back on all the fights, which lasted for days?
I think about how stupid I was were we just crazed.

If only we could have those days again,
So we could spend a little more time together my friend.

But now you are flying high in the sky,
And me, all I do is stand down here and cry.

I miss you so much, you already know,
How could I just stood there and let you go.

Maybe because I know you are coming back,
Knowing that are friendship will not lack.

Understanding and at the same time being very sincere,
And at the same time being proud of you my dear.

For going to school and being on your own,
For showing you can do anything by yourself alone.

But at the same moment I am selfish as ever,
Because I wanted us to be together.

For when the day comes when I need a friend,
Who will I have to turn to then?

And then you come back for a month or two,
Then we have to go through it again me and you.

But this time it will be different you see,
Cause you are moving 4 hours from me.

No more coming over and going out at eat,
No one to call when I feel beat.

Who will give me the support the way you do,
Tell me who is going to be there for you.

Maybe I am just scared that as you move away,
Our friendship will also go astray.

I hope I am wrong and our friendship will grow,
Cause your friendship means more to me than you'll ever know.

As you are away take care my friend,
And if you need advise, I will be there to lend.

A helping hand, a soft shoulder too,
Just remember forever I will be there for you.

TELL ME, TELL ME

Oh tell me, tell me what we should do,
We like the same guy me and you.

One of us might have him that would be great,
If it turns out to be you, remember you I won't hate.

I won't be mean or make fun,
No matter what happens, what's said or done.

I will stick by your side till the end,
No matter what I will be your friend.

I don't know how to explain it or understand why,
But he is a very special guy.

He's got the look and is unique,
Whether it's the way he talks or his physique.

For if you win you won't be my foe,
I'll hold onto his friendship and let the dream go.

FRIENDS

I would like to explain the best way I can,
And that is with paper and pen in hand.

Things started out just as fine as can be,
Then we were friends again you and me.

Then I started calling you everyday,
And we always managed to find something to say.

Then I started hanging around your friends you see,
And I have the feeling you didn't want that to be.

Then it got to the point and pace,
Where we didn't talk when face to face.

Then I said something which I now regret,
Because I shouldn't have gotten mad about people you met.

I left that day and felt hurt too,
Then I started crying because of you.

I wish that you would have not found out,
But that is something I could do nothing about.

Then days pass on like they always do,
And things were different with me and you.

Of course you read the letters that consisted of things you've
known before,
But that day you slammed in my face the door.

I am sure you didn't know it at the time,
Cause the door only slammed in my mind.

Then our big talk took place,
And again tears fell down my face.

Yes, I will admit I did something wrong,
But you don't have to worry about me, I am strong.

I will handle things that come my way,
Even if they turn my sky grey.

I was being honest and serious with you,
When I said if you're happy, I'm happy too.

I am giving you the space in which all friends need,
And I will always be there for you indeed.

There were times, I will say,
When I did want to call you on a certain day.

Just to see if you were alright,
But then I just put the phone down and turned off the light.

I do not want to risk the friendship at hand,
So could you please tell me just where it stands?

Hopefully we still have our friendship you see,
Because that is the most important to me.

A simple question before I go,
Are we still friends yes or no?

JUST REMEMBER

We may not have gotten along the best, that you can't deny,
But still this makes me sad, the moment to say good-bye.

But good-bye means forever and that's along time to part,
So just know you will be thought about often and always in my heart.

We have had some bad times, which I will not say again,
But you know me through it all, I still thought of you as a friend.

Yes, we may not have talked every single day,
But I wish to talk to you now as you go away.

While you are flying high to the place you choose to go,
You are probably thinking of the people you miss so.

But you can bet on one thing that is also true,
Those same people are missing and thinking of you.

So take care of yourself John, and if you are in a tight spot,
Just think back and remember all the friends you got.

Well it is time for me to say bye once again,
And no matter what has happened in the past you are still my
friend.

GOOD FRIENDS

It was great seeing you again,
And it's hard to believe that once we were not friends.
But as we see that has changed,
Because plain and simple, my life I rearranged.
For the good not the bad,
It's hard to believe at you I had gotten mad.
It all seemed so serious then,
I kept saying we would never be friends.
Then one day Dawn left the city,
We missed her though and had some pity.
But then something happened between you and me,
We were like the best of friends, as you can see.
Looking back at all the stupid little fights,
Wondering who was wrong, and who was right.
But it had its moments you must confess,

Remember 5th hour what a mess.

You were there when I had a problem to face,

You always told me how you felt and put me in my place.

And as many times as I have hurt or cried,

Like a true friend you were by my side.

And one thing you taught me, I must admit,

Was to stand up for myself and not to quit.

The good times and bad times I will never forget,

And I will never be sorry that we met.

Because having you as a friend is special to me,

Your friendship means more than money is green.

You stood by my side when I wanted it to end,

And I will always be happy to call you my forever friend.

So as you have figured out by now,

We can get through anything has friends somehow.

And if you ever need a favor I will be here,

Not just to share a friendship but to let you know I care.

Thank you again for being a part of my life,

From the good times, to the sad times and getting through the strife.

I just hope one day I could be,

As good of a friend to you as you have been to me.

DREAMS

I don't know why you won't talk to me,

Maybe you just want me to let you be.

I just want to be friends with you, but you can't see,

You probably think I am doing this just to be me.

Always telling people what to do,
What to say and who to talk to.

Because of my big mouth you now know,
That I like you even though.

I know you don't like me; it's easy to tell,
Because ever since you found out, our friendship has fell.

I wish things could be back like they were then,
When me and you were just friends.

But I realize that can't happen no matter what I do,
Because I really messed it up for me and you.

Not that there was ever a chance for me and you,
But there is always the saying that dreams sometimes come true.

TO A VERY GOOD FRIEND

You wouldn't tell me what to get you; you had to make it tough,
You couldn't make it easy, instead you make it rough.

So for the sake of the thinking that you made me do,
I hope you listen close to what I'm telling you.

Your friendship is dear to me, that you already know,
But now is the time for us to go.

I'm not saying stop being friends, it's not that at all,
I'm not saying the other one won't be able to call.

But we have to face the fact that we may not see each other
again, And I want you to know you will always be my friend.

I'll always be around if you have a problem or two,
I just want to make it clear; I'm always here for you.

And if it comes down to us going our separate ways,
I just ask that you think of me sometimes... okay.

This present symbolizes something that's precious and new,
It is more than just a gift from me to you.

It is something to remind you, of how it use to be,
Always happy and smiling, always there for me.

So before I go I would like to thank you once again,
For being to me a very good friend.

I hope you have a happy graduation and a happy birthday too,
And I want you to know I will never forget you.

THANK YOU SO MUCH

Friendship can mean a lot of things depending on the way you feel,
But one thing I am most certain of is the pain is real.

They'll always be a time or two when you and a friend will fight,
But mainly these little spats last just a few nights.

But I have always been hurt by one of my friends,
And I never thought the pain would end.

I always thought that was how it was suppose to be,
You do things for them and have them do nothing for me.

But sometimes you are lucky to find,
A friendship you're sure will last through time.

The kind of friendship I have found with you,
Always there to see me through.

At first I had doubts you see,
But now I know you're there for me.

No matter if I am happy or sad,
Whether the times are good or bad.

But thanks to you guys I have learned a thing or two,
It's not what you buy or what you do.

The main thing is to be you with no acts at all,
But this will not guarantee the best or stop you when you fall.

But you guys have taught me a lot you see,
Not just to be strong, but to also be me.

So with all my heart I would like to say again,
Thank you so much for being such good friends.

FOR A SPECIAL FRIEND

You have helped me with problems, you were always there,
No matter what, you always cared.
You cheered me up when I was down,
No matter how sad, you were always around.
And I would like to thank you again,
For being to me a special friend.
I hope you birthday is full of laughs and fun times too,
Just answer one question; you won't forget me, will you?
For I have only met you a few months ago,
And how special you are to me that you'll never know.

FALLING APART

As the end is closing near,
All the thoughts are not as clear.

Not as many fun times, just a few,
Hardly any memories of me and you.

No more times of talks or calls,
Nothing really between us at all.

What has happened? A good question at last,
Can you tell what's gone wrong in the past?

Or is it me thinking to long,
Just looking for something to say is wrong.

I am confused; don't want to see the light,
Because I am scared this time I may be right.

That something happened to bad to mend,
And that me and you are no longer friends.

To me it seems you can no longer trust,
And to have a friendship that is a must.

Of all the times we would disagree,
No matter what you were there for me.

And I know you are still there,
If I need to talk to someone I know cares.

But you have been acting like I am not there for you,
And I want you to know that's not true.

No matter whom my other friends may be,
No one has been there like you are for me.

But to you, my loyalty will always stay,
And it will last forever and a day.

So please remember that in the end,
No matter what I am always your friend.

Tracey Pizzino

MY BEST FRIEND

I may not show it all the time,
But the best of friend in you did I find.

We have good times and some bad,
And always those make us sad.

But the good times we will always know,
Even when it is time for us to let go.

We will have to try to get along alone,
So when we are out on our own.

But each other I will never forget,
That is one thing you can bet.

No more fights, no more tears,
No more arguments through the years.

No more heartaches, no more pain,
Just happiness to keep us sane.

We will remember this year with some fun we shared,
And always will know that the other cared.

We will see each others problems through,
So that the skies will be no longer grey but a beautiful blue.

I think we have both learned a lesson from this,
It is something like your very first kiss.

That happens once before it is gone,
So pick your friends and don't be wrong.

They say you can get a boyfriend any day of the week,
But a very special friend is tough to find and keep.

And that is what I have found in you,
A special person who I feel is true.

No matter if my feelings could be erased,
No one could ever take your place.

And if I may say it again,
This is why you are my best friend.

TIL DEATH DO US PART

We made it through another year,
Through all the pain and the tears.

We managed to put the past to rest,
We finally realized what was best.

We are still together as best friends you see,
Just like we said you and me.

Always joking and speaking our minds,
This friendship I guarantee will last through time.

Tracey Pizzino

You want me to tell you how I know,
Well listen close cause here I go.

First we got along great,
Each other we could never hate.

Then all of a sudden we always had a problem or two,
It was either me or it was you.

Then with each other we would have fights,
But it would only last for two nights.

Then we became closer together,
And promised to let nothing come between us ever.

Now we tell the other what's on our mind,
This is how I know it will last through time.

But in the summer will be a blast,
We can think about the present and the future and forget the past.

But when it comes times for you to go,
My life will turn from fast pace to slow.

But I will manage until you come back,
And I promise our friendship won't even lack.

It will just grow stronger through the letters,
And it won't be worse but a lot better.

So when you come back it will be like the start,
But we'll be together forever till death do us part.

CAN YOU PICTURE

Can you picture the sky is blue, but then turned to grey,
Can you picture our lasting friendship that slowly faded away?

Can you picture the birds that fly as free as can be?
Can you picture how much hurt inside you have caused me.

Can you picture the days gone by as just a thing of the past,
Or can you picture the mistakes we made will have made us learn
at last.

Can you picture a second chance for us, will come around again,
Can you picture you and me as ever becoming friends?

Can you picture the good times we had as well as the bad,
Can you picture a brother figure that made me so sad?

Can you picture finally why I did it now?
Can you understand I had to help somehow?

Now as I am done with you,
I'll tell you what I am going to do.

I have asked you questions that consist of me,
Now I will tell you what I see.

I see the birds that fly so high,
Floating freely through the sky.

I can see the past as though it was today,
I can see the mistakes we made along the way.

I see our friendship losing its glow,
Just as you see of melting snow.

I can see us being friends one day,
When--- well that I cannot say.

I WONDER IF...

I wonder if you care at all,
If I succeed or if I fall.

I wonder if you know or see,
Just how much you mean to me.

I wonder if it failed to show,
Of just how much our friendship did grow.

I wonder if you feel bad,
When you step on people and make them sad.

I wonder if you'll ever grow up and learn,
That playing with fire will only get you burned.

I wonder how you feel today,
Are you happy or very grey?

Are you wondering at all you see?
Of just how much you have hurt me.

Or don't you really even care,
That the friendship we once had isn't all there.

Or maybe this is your way to show,
That our friendship is one thing you wish to let go.

Fine if that's how you want it to be,
But I wonder if you were ever really a friend to me.

THIS ONE'S FOR YOU

I have never wrote a poem for you,
It maybe sad, but very true.

And you have done so much for me,
You let me see things the way they should be.

And when I was sad or hurt in some way,
You were always there to brighten my day.

Always around when I was glad,
Even there if I was sad.

Tracey Pizzino

Always looking at the good,
Saying things can go away if I only could.

Let them go and stay in the past,
Forget them and live my life at last.

Remember the good and forget the rest,
We both knew that would be best.

But you knew me and what I did,
I had to play it like a kid.

Hang around to see if things would change,
But instead my life got rearranged.

But still you stood by me, always forever,
And even when we were fighting we were somehow together.

Sure we have had our share,
But no matter what we knew the other cared.

And if for some reason we just had to talk something out,
We knew the other would be there without a doubt.

Well that seems long ago now,
And we are still friends again somehow.

So as you can see we have been through a lot,
And no matter what I say, I have never forgot.

I know our friendship will never lack,
Because we have been to hell and back.

And we saw our problems through together,
And said we would be friends forever.

And there is one more thing I wish to do,
And that is to say this one's for you.

WHAT WILL HAPPEN TO OUR FRIENDSHIP

Can you tell me what will happen when we go our separate ways?
Will it be in the past under one of those days?

Will it die more and more with each passing year?
Until it is wiped away just like a tear.

Or will it just be a faded memory in your mind,
That eventually will be forgotten in time.

Maybe it will be pushed back until needed again,
I doubt that seriously because we are friends.

But I thank you for believing in me and teaching me to trust again,
Cause it took me a lot to confide in a friend.

So tell me what will happen to our friendship, when graduation comes and goes,
Will it still last forever or melt away like snow.

Tracey Pizzino

THIS TIME I KNOW

Me and you friends again, that's how I wanted it to be,
No one hurt or sad you see.

Only happy, better than before,
No matter what was behind the door.

I looked over everything that you guys said and done,
I accepted your apologizes and thought I'd won.

But at the same time you thought you had won too,
And again I would fall like I sometimes do.

I wanted this friendship to be strong like the past,
But I only thought of the good times the ones that will last.

But I thought about something, in which I have done time and time again,
I always had to convince myself that you were my friend.

I shouldn't have to convince myself of friends you see,
Because then they are not true friends to be.

We had good times and I will never forget,
But now I feel the worst thing was the day we met.

You seemed so nice, to good to be true,
No matter what, there for me were you.

Then something happened and the niceness went away,
And for about three months my sky went grey.

For I thought my world had come to an end,
And all because of a couple of friends.

Then better things did become,
We were talking and telling of the things we had done.

But again I tired to make the friendship something I knew could
never be,
I tired to make us the best of friends again, you and me.

And again you hurt me, but this time so small,
But I promise you this time I will not fall.

Fall into the little games you play,
Believing all you have done for me or all that you say.

The last thing I ever wanted was to let go,
For I thought we would last forever, not melt away like snow.

Because the truth was all I ever asked, whether good or bad,
For that is the best way to go, even if it makes you sad.

Yes, it will hurt me to say good-bye to you,
But this time I know it's something I must do.

Tracey Pizzino

SPECIAL

You have done so much for me, you're always there,
When I have a problem, you always care.

You taught me how to trust again,
How to confide in a friend.

To not believe what people say?
To talk things out, not walk away.

And as you know, I help my friends,
I don't care what the consequences maybe in the end.

And for us the end is drawing near,
But your friendship to me is very dear.

So if by chance we go our separate ways,
And don't talk to each other for days.

Because of the memories in our minds,
I guarantee our friendship will last through time.

And if we lose touch for some reason at all, it maybe sad but true,
There will always be someone special to me, and that person is
you.

DRUG DEALER

I told you it would happen alright,
I just didn't know what day or night.

But I thought you would have got caught by another,
Like maybe a cop or even a brother.

But I never dreamed of this much trouble,
That the last thing you would see was a barrel, (double).

Because of the loss I can only try,
To hold onto memories, for they can't die.

No one can take them away,
They won't get lost or go astray.

They will be with me until the end of time,
Just like I had hoped for a friend of mine.

You couldn't just stop; you had to prove it,
Life is nothing without money so you had to do it.

But that is where your last mistake came in,
You never thought you were going to lose, but always win.

Well I hope you are proud of what you have done,
Because one thing is for certain you haven't won.

In fact you pushed it to the edge, to the line,
And all of us thought it was going fine.

I know you can't read this, for you are not here,
But I hope you know your friendship was very dear.

One thing I will say, you always cared for your friends,
But your priorities got mixed up and then it ends.

But it didn't stop with just you,
Cause part of us died too.

SYMBOLIZES

A friend is someone who is always there,
Always around to show they care.

Always happy when you are blue,
Glad they are friends with you.

But sometimes for no reason at all,
You just wish they didn't call.

And when they don't you get mad,
Saying it's their fault you are sad.

But I finally got tired of my little ways,
And to you I promise to stop today.

You have been a good friend to me I'll admit,
And you were there telling me not to quit.

You understand why I do the things I do,
And I am happy to be friends with you.

But there is one thing I always want you to remember,
Not just now, this is forever.

I buy my friends things so that in the end,
They can look back and remember that I was their friend.

Cause candy and money just fades away,
And I want my friends to remember me for more than a day.

So I guess the bear meant just a little more,
Then I thought it did when I bought it before.

It means to me, that no matter what I may do,
I will hopefully always be a friend to you.

NO MATTER WHAT

No matter what was done or said,
No matter what went through my head.
No matter what the past is gone,
No matter what I stayed strong.
No matter what will come to be,
You will always have a friend in me.
No matter what the future has in store,
No matter what is behind the door.
No matter what, people think or say,
No matter what, I understand anyway.

No matter what I will always care,

No matter what I am always there.

No matter what has happened or may come to be,

You will always have a friend, me!!

There were some bad times but also some good,

I hate to say it, but I should.

You have hurt me, I won't lie,

And believe you me, I more than once cried.

ALL BECAUSE OF YOU

All the times I wanted to just give up and hide,
You were right there by my side.

Telling me not to give up and show them they won,
You were always there through thick and thin, no matter what I've done.

You really don't care if I am thin or fat,
You like me the same and that is that.

You don't care if they get mad at you because of me,
You told me I was you friend to stay and that's how it would be.

I am glad you are my friend, that's what you say,
And I will remember that day by day.

But most of all when I am down,
When the days come and I just want to frown.

I will remember the times you were there for me,
But promise to open my eyes and see.

That I don't need them as a friend,
Because I am the one that came out winning in the end.

FRIENDSHIP

The friendship we have is fresh and new,
And from the time it started this friendship grew.

Little problems arose every now and then,
But we still managed to stay friends.

No matter what, we saw it through,
Together like a team me and you.

Always with each other every step of the way,
Clearing up the skies that once were gray.

Helping each other with things that came about,
When one of us was in need or had a doubt.

The friendship we have is not unjust,
Because we have the special ingredient and that is trust.

I hope this friendship continues to stay,
As strong as it is at this moment today.

Tracey Pizzino

WHAT IS A BEST FRIEND

Well it is someone who shares,
And someone who cares.

Someone to laugh with and share a tear,
Someone who is there for more than a year.

Someone who knows your good points and your faults too,
Someone who loves you for just being you.

Someone who listens when you need a friend,
Someone who sticks by you till the end.

For even if they are not there everyday,
They are always by you somehow, someway.

Whether it is in the heart or mind,
These are the very rarest to find.

For you were always there when I needed you the most,
And to our special friendship I give a toast.

To the one who has been there for me till the end?
With honors I call you my best friend.

ONLY TIME CAN TELL

I finally got what I wanted, to let you know I'm there,
I'll always be your friend to sympathize and care.

I'll always have the memories of how it use to be,
When I needed to talk and you were there for me.

I'll always remember the fun times that we had,
And yet still recall the sad.

I will always hold on to things in my heart,
Like the friendship we had at the start.

Maybe in time things will work out,
But will we still always have this doubt.

That things could be different if we watch what we say,
We could even be friends today.

The way it is now and the way it was then,
But yet it doesn't have to end.

Maybe in time we will make amends,
And you and I will be friends.

IT IS OVER

When I think things are going fine,
The memories come flowing back to mind.

The laughs and the fun times we had,
And all the memories of the bad.

I still wonder what happened what went wrong,
For our friendship was stable and very strong.

We could talk about anything whenever you called,
Now we don't have anything to say at all.

We did have fights every now and then,
But we managed to stay friends.

Maybe since this is your last year things will be fine,
As long as I can erase you all from my mind.

It will take some time, this I know,
But for some of the memories I will never let go.

LETTING GO

One day I knew we would have to say good-bye and go our
separate ways,
And just think back to the good old days.

I hope you have happiness in the days to come,
And conquer the obstacles one by one.

I will always remember the good times we had,
And never let those memories make me sad.

We did have a lot of times of regret,
But I am glad that we met.

Maybe in the future we will meet again,
And be able to call each other friend.

There is a lot more I have to say,
But I can't seem to find a way.

I will always have the memories of the fights and talks,
The playing tennis and the taking walks.

But times change as we both know,
And the hardest part is the letting go.

But in the future maybe friend,
We will have the chance to meet again.

I DON'T HATE HER

Our friendship faded and I know why,
When she walked into the picture you said good-bye.

She still talks to me and tells me what is wrong,
My friendship with her is still strong.

I don't hate her for anything she has done,
But hopefully you she has not won.

Today will tell me the real reason why,
Whether it was you or because of her that you said good-bye.

Tracey Pizzino

Hopefully we can stay friends and even talk now and then,
Just as long as you don't say that's it's, the end.

Today I will wait for the phone to ring,
And try to explain everything.

I hope you tell me how you really feel,
And tell me our friendship is worth the time to heal.

That even though we made mistakes,
That our friendship won't be the fate.

That we can work all this out,
And we'll have our friendship back with no more doubts.

Please don't get me wrong,
I hope you two last forever just like a song.

But even songs add a new tune now and then,
And you new tunes will be your friends.

So I hope you two will learn to see,
That with each other you can't always be.

So each of you should have friends,
People that will be there for you in the end.

Boy or girl why should you care,
Just knowing someday that they'll be there.

It should make you proud when in a tight spot,
Looking back and seeing all the friends you got.

FEBRUARY 23, 1987

I called you last night to see if we could talk,
And down memory lane did we walk.

Not with our feet, but in our minds,
We took this walk for an hour's time.

We talked about the future, present and past,
About things that ended and things we hope will last.

I am glad that I did not listen to my friends,
Who said not to call you ever again?

But I knew you would always be there if I need to talk,
No matter if it is from my head or my heart.

When problems arise and I have to straighten them out,
You are there beyond all doubt.

Listening to whatever I have to say,
Clearing up the skies that were dull that day.

We still can talk about anything at all,
And I proved it yesterday when I called.

For awhile I thought our friendship was through,
But I am glad you said we were still friends again me and you.

THE END RESULT

I don't know how it started, I try but can't recall,
How it came about an all.

Yet I'll try the best I can,
And that is with pen and paper in hand.

To remember the steps and the days,
What was done and in what ways.

You started out as our waiter, so pleasant and kind,
You seemed so polite and care free, nothing on your mind.

Then we started asking for you whenever we went out,
You were the best, without a doubt.

Then we started talking just a little more,
But it was different than before.

Not like a waiter to customer, but friend to friend,
Some things didn't have to be said for us to comprehend.

You have been so nice and kind, you always seem to be,
When I need a friend to talk to, there you are for me.

We talked about our problems and try to help each other out,
Mostly when one of us seems to have a doubt.

I'm glad to have met you, and had the chance to know you well,
But there is something, you, I wish to tell.

I couldn't imagine anyone in all my day,
Like you, who always, to me, had a kind word to say?

You have come along way in school and I'm proud of you,
Yet there still are a few years left, but I know you'll make it through.

And if it ever gets to the point where you need a hand,
A shoulder, a listener, or someone to understand.

I'll always only be a phone call away,
Because for all you have done for me, the favor I'll repay.

I'll always be there to help, no questions asked at all,
And I'll even be there if one day you fall.

Well that's how it started or at least what I remember,
I just never thought the end result, would be, a friend forever.

TOO MANY FACES

Too many faces, too many lies,
Too many what ifs, too many whys.

Tracey Pizzino

Too many I'm sorry' I won't do it again,
Too many that's what you got me for friend.

Not enough honesty to say listen here,
It's not because I don't, I really do care.

It's not enough anything, nothings the same,
I make up the rules as I play the game.

The faces, the tempers, the mood swings too,
It all looks so much different to you.

Like I change my emotion in a blink of an eye,
But that's not the true me, it's all a lie.

It took along time to perfect my defense you see,
It allows me the protection, yet lets me be me.

My guards always up, but my masks change shape,
Nothing can go into another ones place.

You must be exact to not show the signs,
You must think all the while, with your mind.

To go from happy to sad, or pissed to pain,
Comes with no loses and has no gains.

It's like a turtle's shell, to secure and protect,
Like a neat little file cabinet, so you don't forget.

The only flaw this thinking bares,
Is one that none of you can share.

I totally see things differently than you,
Something that your understanding will never do.

None of you would say this, but that's not the case,
Yet something that stares me in the face.

Actions and words can hurt more than anything else,
But it's thinking alone, I caused pain to myself.

Mood swings are good they let people be free,
Mostly when I no longer what to be me.

I can be anyone I want to, act nice or mean,
And all the emotions that come between.

But no matter how I'm acting I never stop being friends,
That is something that will last to the end.

So no matter how many phrases I go through,
I will never stop caring about any of you.

THE TRUE MEANING

The meaning of the word friend does not to justice for you,
No matter what came my way, you helped me through.

Tracey Pizzino

You were always giving advice, or lending me an ear,
When ever times were good or bad, you were always there.

You made me laugh when I wanted to frown,
You picked me up when I was down.

You had faith in me when I had doubts,
You were always there to bail me out.

You gave everything you could, and taught me how to stand,
On my own and hope they would understand.

You never doubted me; you never turned to leave,
Everything was a lesson on how to excel an achieve.

But now your time has come to move on, to be better than before,
Your horizon is wider now, and you must open a new door.

I'm happy and I'm sad, I'm grateful and blue,
But no matter what just know I'll miss you.

I'm proud of what you are doing, and I'll support you to the end,
For you have taught me the true meaning of the word friend.

You helped me open my eyes, when I couldn't see at all,
And you always seemed to be right there just before a fall.

I'll never forget the advice, the good times or the cries,
But now it is time for us to say good-bye.

I hope you keep in touch and take care of yourself each and everyday,
And just know one thing my friend, in my heart you'll always stay.

YOU ARE

A friend who was there when I was done,
A friend who made me smile instead of frown.

A friend who stuck by me through all of the pain,
A friend like you is to me a gain.

A friend who listened to my sorrows,
A friend who I talked to about my tomorrows.

A friend I have known for three years,
A friend who I told to my hopes and fears.

You know my good side and my bad,
And at times we made the other mad.

But through these years you have taught me a lot,
And even through the aches and pains I have never forgot.

But now it is time for letting go,
For you to leave, live and grow.

There is one question in which comes to mind,
Will our friendship last through time?

Tracey Pizzino

Part of me says yes, the other no,
Part of me says hang on, the other let go.

I have already done what I planned to do,
And answered my question, yes, our friendship is true.

I thank you again for always being there,
For helping and showing you do care.

My dream came true this I now know,
It just took time and progressed slow.

So remember one thing on your graduation day,
Dreams do come true, somehow, someway.

TO GOOD TO LAST

It is over done with through,
I am finally going to give up on you.

Our friendship I now know will never last,
It won't be the way it was in the past.

I'm tired of counting the tries,
When I forgave you for all the lies.

In the future I hope you learn,
But if you don't boy will you get burned.

I hope you know that I did care,
And will remember the secrets we did share.

When we called each other when we were blue,
When we needed cheering up or someone to talk to.

But now I am finally aware of your game,
And unlike your other friends, I won't be put to shame.

Maybe as time passes you will see what you did,
For you have to grow up sooner or later and stop being a kid.

For all your little games will hurt you in the end,
When you look around and see not one friend.

But hopefully you will see, before it's too late,
That you have to talk things out instead of just hate.

For I once thought this friendship was held by ties,
Not a bunch of your stupid lies.

I told you I just couldn't go through this again,
I never wanted to think of you as a fake friend.

But I guess you thought I would play along,
But for once you are so very wrong.

I will tell you one thing which is true,
No matter how much we have hurt each other, I will never forget
you.

We had some great times, but too many bad,
And I just can't seem to forget all we had.

And I do hate to see this end,
Because at one time we were great friends.

But until you stop just thinking of you,
As far as right now this friendship is through.

AT THE START

At the start are friendship was strong,
But as time passed we found it was wrong.

We talked about stuff that sometimes surprised me,
We were like the best of friends and that was how it would be.

But little problems always came about,
Then we started having doubts.

Whether this was going to come to an end or continue forever,
If we were going to stay friends and see everything through
together.

Last summer things didn't go so great,
Because me, your brother and friends did hate.

All the times I called to talk on the phone,
Your brother just hung up and said you weren't home.

Most of the time it was true,
You weren't there, this I knew.

But this summer I won't stand around anymore,
For me to try and talk to you and them slamming the doors.

No matter how much I want our friendship to last,
I can't live my future like I lived my past.

I don't want to pretend we hate each other,
Just to please your friends and brother.

To talk only when they are gone,
Because our friendship use to be better than that and twice as
strong.

So for the sake of how I feel,
To me our friendship was a steal.

And in the beginning I thought it would never end,
For I thought of you as my forever friend.

I will miss you more than I can say,
And I will think of you with each passing day.

But I don't think you still want to try,
So please have manners and just say good-bye.

Tracey Pizzino

MY FRIEND

My friend, you were so bold,
My friend, a loving hand to hold.

My friend, so very kind and dear,
My friend, you were always near.

My friend, was brave and true,
My friend, this is for you.

My friend, who made me laugh and sing,
My friend, I'd talk to when the phone did ring.

My friend, I didn't want this to end,
And hopefully in the future it will be again.

I am sorry this wasn't meant to be,
Because there is no more my friend and me.

GOOD-BYE

I am glad we are friends again and that is how it's going to stay,
No matter what they do or even say.

Maybe we should stop talking but just for awhile,
So they can just sit back and smile.

I never wanted it to end up like this,
But it ended up the way they wanted and that's all there is.

But I will never let go of the good times we had,
I will promise you they will never make me sad.

But I don't want them to get mad at you,
And we know this is something we should do.

I did everything I could Kristy, I really did try,
But so they don't get mad at you I think we should say good-bye.

YOU ARE THERE

You were always there when I needed you,
When I needed to talk or felt blue.

You helped me with everything that came my way,
In fact you are still doing that today.

You are there if something goes wrong,
Telling me to stay strong.

And even if you are away somewhere,
Something tells me that you still care.

You are always thinking of your friends,
Trying to make amends.

I hope you never forget me, because I won't forget you,
And that is what I call a true friend true.

Tracey Pizzino

WHY GOD GAVE US FRIENDS

Someone to understand us when we are blue,
Someone to help us all year through.

Someone to listen to what we say,
Someone who is there everyday.

Friends help us through things that may come,
And help make sure we get them done.

So now we know what friends do,
They are here to help me and you.

People that stick with us till the end,
And that is why God gave us friends.

JUST A FRIEND

I like you so much I wish you knew,
I wish there was something I could do.
Like write you a letter or call on the phone,
Just to see if you are home.
Maybe you would write or even talk,
Or would want to go for a walk.
But that is something I can't do,
I can't tell anyone I like you.
So it will remain like it's been,
You will be just a friend.

BEST FRIEND FOREVER

You are my best friend now and forever,
And we'll stay that way even if we are not together.

For if things should happen and we should part,
You will always be in my heart.

I guess this is the time to go our separate ways,
But for long my skies will be grey.

I hope you are happy and make new friends,
As long as you don't say our friendship must end.

One thing is for certain how hard I must try,
Please promise me you won't ever say good-bye.

A FRIEND

You kept telling me to leave it alone,
But I had to find out on my own.

That I did everything all wrong,
Because I wanted to belong.

But then I realized that it was not you,
Because you guys don't like people just for what they do.

You like people for what they are,
Not for money, homework, or their car.

It took me a long time to see,
That you guys were always there for me.

But as they say in the end,
Life is nothing without a friend.

But now I can see,
That is what all of you are to me.
     A FRIEND!!!

THE FRIENDSHIP YOU GAVE ME

You guys were the best anyone ever had,
I am sorry that I made you all so sad.

I wish I could take back everything I ever said,
Maybe I would have been better off dead.

But no matter what happened in the past,
I know one thing that will always last.

That is something in my heart,
That was there from the start.

I will never forget, but I hope you can see,
I will always have the friendship you gave me.

OPINIONS

You said they were stupid, you said they were wrong,
You said they are not good for me, that they don't belong.

They will use or hurt me in someway,
They are just playing with my head from day to day.

I said they were different and they were my friends,
In time of need they would be there once again.

They have never used or hurt me the way some others did,
I grew up in the past two years; I am no longer a kid.

They make me believe in myself and taught me how to trust again,
And no matter what you say, they are my friends.

You spoke your opinion and how you felt,
But I am the one who has to handle the cards that were dealt.

I may sometimes seem ungrateful or very blue,
But I haven't forgotten you have done a lot for me too.

I am not trying to judge you or make you mad,
I am just trying not to be sad.

So now I hope you understand just a little bit better,
And I know that it won't last forever.

But in the end it always works out best,
And soon this problem will be put to rest.

But I will have the memories of their friendship through time,
And be proud to look back and say they were friends of mine.

But for me and you this I do not have to say,
Because I know our friendship will last forever and a day.

DIDN'T WANT TO SAY GOOD-BYE

I have to get over you, but it's not going so great,
No matter what you did, you I just can't hate.

When I saw you, all I wanted to do was say hi,
But no matter what I can only say good-bye.

I have all these memories I just can't get out of my mind,
For I thought our friendship would last through time.

I still wonder if you are okay and safe,
If everything is fine or out of it's place.

I know this is for the best,
But the memories of our friendship I can't put to rest.

But what about me, you said you cared,
And the inner most secrets with me you shared.

Why did this all have to end?
When we were really good friends.

Time after time I asked you to tell me the truth,
I didn't ask for your life just your youth.

So tell me please, was your brother right,
Did you stay my friend so I wouldn't be hurt or uptight?

Tim, I called on the phone to say good-bye,
So you wouldn't see the tears in my eyes.

You hurt me more than you'll ever know,
And the hardest part was when I let go.

IT'S NOT

It's not like we're fighting,
It's not like we're mad.
It's not like we're wondering if the other is sad.
It's not like we see things,
It's not like we're blue.
It's not like we miss the me and you.
It's not like we're talking,
It's not that at all.
It's not like we're waiting for the other one to call.
It's not that it's happy like it use to be,
It's not like the friendship of you and me.
It's not like we're enemies, but then again,
That's not it at all, we're just not friends.

Tracey Pizzino

WE MAY HAVE OUR DIFFERENCES

You may have problems here and there,
But always remember that I care.

You may not want to talk but you just might,
And if you do I'm there for you day or night.

We may have had our differences in the past,
But always I knew this friendship would last.

And I am glad, me, you have learned to trust,
Because to have a special friendship that is a must.

So if anything is on your mind,
Just remember for you I'm easy to find.

I'll help you in anyway I can,
So that your future will be just grand.

We'll get through whatever may come,
Because right now you're my top priority, #1.

Just to call you a friend would be a lie,
For you are my best friend and this is why.

You have always been there for me,
But that is easy and plain to see.

You have helped me when I felt down,
You were there to lift up my frown.

You were there when I wanted my life to end,
And forever to me you are my best friend.

And I'll promise you something that has been proven true,
There's nothing in the world that we can't do.

And along the way there'll be good and bad,
But we can't let that get us frustrated or sad.

We have to stick together and stay strong,
And with you at my side we can't go wrong.

And believe me; this will take more than a day,
But we'll figure something out, somehow, someway.

TO ME, FRIENDS ALWAYS

I thought you were my friend, or at least that is what you said,
Now you just sit there and tilt back your head.

You think I just hate you, and would leave you be,
But if that is the case then you really didn't know me.

I can't hate you, not then or now,
I promise we will be talking again soon somehow.

I won't let you leave, not without a fight,
Because no matter what you think this time you're not right.

Tracey Pizzino

And if by chance it is really through,
I will never forget the person I knew.

Because the person I knew was nice and kind,
A caring person who spoke his mind.

I don't understand what made you change,
But my life you rearranged.

So now all I can do is to still try,
Because I can't let go or say good-bye.

But please know that in the end,
No matter what has happened to me, you will always be my friend.

SUCH GOOD FRIENDS

Whatever happened to the good times, no one hurt, no one sad,
All those days are over, now we are mad.

Someone said something that was not what it seemed,
Then I realized this make believe friendship was all a dream.

All the doubts that came along,
And you saying they were wrong.

Now they are proven to be true,
Just like him and me, but now it's me and you.

What happened to the friendship of you and me?

Please don't tell me it wasn't meant to be.

For if that is true and all this was a lie,
I can only try not to cry.

People were against it from the start,
But it had a different kind of heart.

It had a way that seemed so right,
Now I am having doubts on this cold night.

But I just can't help but remember that line,
This one will last through time.

I set myself up for the fall,
Now I have to try and forget it all.

But remember one thing that has not happened yet,
I forgive anything, I just never forget.

Maybe you have a good reason for being mad,
But look already, you're even, I'm sad.

Can't we go back to the way it was then?
Me and you such good friends.

THE HIGHEST COST

I had the feeling things would mend,
And go to the way it was back then.

Tracey Pizzino

When me and you first met,
Now that is one thing I will never forget.

Things were the best they could be,
We were getting along great you and me.

Then things stated to fall apart,
And it wasn't like we had in the start.

But we managed to see most of the problems through,
We survived it and that we knew.

But I guess things got out of control,
Because our friendship lost its heart and soul.

Again we tried to make amends,
And have me and you still remain friends.

It worked for just a little while,
Then between us came the miles.

All of the things have hurt me so,
And I never wanted to let it go.

It feels like I finally lost,
But I had to pay with the highest cost.

The friendship that meant the most to me,
Why couldn't Mike just let us be?

MY FRIEND AND ME

My friend so very bold,
My friend a loving hand to hold.

My friend so kind and dear,
My friend you were always near.

My friend so brave and true,
My friend this is for you.

My friend no matter what will come,
My friend you were the only one.

The one I could trust with no fear,
And brought to my eyes a single tear.

I wish it could have continued to grow,
But what our friendship meant to me, you'll never know.

It ended as we can see,
Because there is no more my friend and me.

A FRIEND LIKE YOU

A word said so frequently, yet no one seems to care,
That just using the word, does not mean it's there.

Tracey Pizzino

The word I am referring to is "friend" you see,
And this is the difference between them and me.

I do not use it carelessly, like every time I say hi,
I do not say everyone I know is my friend, why.

A simple word, yet so complex, the meaning ever changed,
From something good and special, then totally rearranged.

For it takes a certain quality, that makes one a friend,
Someone to share the good and bad, and cry with now and then.

Someone who can see your flaws and like you all the same,
For someone who is always willing to talk, before placing the blame.

I don't know how this started, or how it came to be,
All I know is now, you are friends with me.

Who said the first word, I really can't recall,
Who started the first conversation is anyone's call.

The one thing I do know is how rare it is to find,
People, whom you just met, yet feel you knew all the time.

You're funny, easy going, polite and very kind,
Yet you don't have a problem with speaking your mind.

Sure we may have acquaintances, people we see now and then,
Yet truthfully looking close, do we have that many friends.

People that will stick by you, no matter what may be,
Someone who in a bad situation, yet the good they only see.

To take you at your word, to believe what you say,
To always have faith and never walk away.

Friends start out as strangers, then a word is said,
And in front of us we start to pave the road ahead.

Through curves and hills, valleys and plains,
From something so understandable, to almost insane.

No matter what the reason, people come and go,
Only a handful can be called a friend, this we always know.

No one knows where life will lead us, or how long we will stay,
In the place that we are today.

Though we may not see each other for weeks, months or years,
I will only be a phone call away should you have some fears.

No matter what the reason, no matter what the time,
A friend in me, you will always find.

For this is one thing above the rest,
To me, my friends, deserve the best.

So as I go to end this, remember this is true,
I am very lucky to have found a friend like you.

Tracey Pizzino

FOREVER FRIENDS

Our friendship is strong and stable,
Because we are willing and very able.

To see anything at all through,
Always together and hardly blue.
We can talk about anything or anyone,
No matter whom it is or what they've done.

You are always there for us, as we are for you,
But sometimes we say things that aren't true.

But no matter what the situation we managed fine,
To hold on to our friendship the whole time.

And just to prove we mean what we say,
Just remember these next lines everyday.

No one will come between us being friends,
Unless one of us dies then it will end.

But until that time finally comes around,
We will help you never to feel down.

So if you ever need to talk about anyone at all,
Please promise us you'll pick up the phone and call.

Because no matter what, we will always be there,
Giving you advice, listening or just telling you we care.

So just have fun in the days to come,

Because we were given life but only one.

So live it to the most you can,
It maybe sad, okay, or just grand.

And down some roads it may seem hard,
But just go down with your confidence on guard.

And no matter what you will always win,
Just tilt your head back and stick up that chin.

For things will always turn out,
Even if along the way there are hundreds of doubts.

Just stick to what you feel is right,
And don't let anyone get you uptight.

For after you have put your mind to it,
There is nothing in the world to stop you from doing it.

And our friendship, we promise, will continue to stay,
The very same way it is today.

And that is why until the end,
We can say you are, our forever friend.

FRIENDS, FOREVER

Things aren't going very well,
It seems to me our friendship has fell.

I wish we were talking like we use to,
You calling me and me calling you.

But I guess our friendship was never meant to be,
Because I have the feeling you can't stand me.

I am sorry if I said anything to put you in a bind,
To make you think like this and change your mind.

I wish we would have stayed friends,
But the way things are it looks like the end.

Because I know your friends don't want you to talk to me,
So I guess I will just let you be.

I hope you understand I will always be your friend,
But they are the ones that want it to end.

But I will always be here if you need to talk,
And if they don't like that then they can take a walk.

But before I leave I just had to say,
I still think of you as my friend till this day.

ARE WE STILL FRIENDS

I can't believe it happened to me,
Not just one or two times but three.

I wish you never would have found out,
It would have been better that way, beyond all doubt.

Your friendship means more to me than I can say,
You said I could talk to you, night or day.

But now I don't know what to do,
Should I stop calling or still talk to you.

I am sorry for all I have done,
I feel like I messed up another one.

I hope you are happy and succeed in everything you do,
I hope you will still think of me as your friend too.

Before I go there's one more thing,
If you ever need to talk just give me a ring.

SORRY I FORGOT

I knew you didn't like me, that was easy to see,
I just wanted to be friends, but that could never be.

Yes, we still talk, but not like before,
You don't seem to call as much anymore.

You say "I will call back", and you say it a lot,
But you always find an excuse and say "I forgot".

Well that line doesn't work anymore,
And even when you do call it's only because you're bored.

Well this year things will change a lot,
And I will be the one saying, "Sorry I forgot".

I CAN REMEMBER

The good times and bad times too,
But most of all when I was blue.

When you made me laugh and cry,
When we talked and I told you if she was worth it try.

I made mistakes but really can't recall,
What any of them had to do with you at all?

I tried once more to become your friend,
But people told me it was the end.

No matter how you act now, I will never forget,
The way it was when first we met.

I will never forget the friendship we had,
Even if the memories make me sad.

FRIENDS ARE FOREVER

Friends are forever and this we all know,
And no matter where you are we will never let go.

Because of you leaving we have lost a lot,
But we have the memories and we have not forgot.

We miss you more than words can say,
And maybe we will see each other someday.

One thing is for certain no matter what we do,
No one will ever be able to take the place of you.

SO, MY FRIEND

You make people happy if they are sad,
And at your friends you never get mad.

Always around when we need you the most,
And to our friendship I will toast.

That no matter how old I may become,
I will always be proud of you for what you have done.

The memories of our childhood seem so clear,
Times of happiness, times of fear.

So with the memories I have in my mind,
I see friends like you are the rarest to find.

So my friend, no matter if you are far away,
Just know in my heart you'll always stay.

FRIENDS AGAIN

Now we are friends and that is how it's going to stay,

Now and forever starting today.

When I thought we weren't friends all I did was cry,

I felt like all I wanted to do was die.

But I will always be here for you, if something goes wrong,

To help you through it and keep you strong.

You can always count on me to help you with whatever may come,

Because I will help you fight the obstacles one by one.

People kept telling me to forget we were friends,

They said it had to stop, come to an end.

I told them no, I didn't care what I had to do,

We were going to be friends again me and you.

WE THOUGHT YOU
WERE OUR FRIEND

I thought you were our friend, but I guess I was wrong,

I thought you were a person, but you're just a song.

You needed a place to start, and a place to end.

You needed us to be your friend.

Well we fell for it like you knew we would,

You sang the song the way you should.

But it was all a lie, no matter how hard we tried,

To convince ourselves other wise.

Your using us now like you used us then,

Trying to make us think you were our friend.

LET GO OF YOU

What to do if you are down,
Just be happy and don't frown.
Because it never helps and won't do,
So I have to just give up on you.
I guess our friendship is over for good,
I just wish things were back to the way it should.
No more heartache, no more tears,
No more waiting what seems like years.
Just us talking getting things straightened out,
Getting rid of all these doubts.
People don't know how I feel for that I cannot do,
So it will have to be up to me to get over you.
I hope you find someone who is kind and dear,
But just remember my love for you will last through the years.
I can't forget or even start to erase,
All the memories I cannot face.
One day this will seem so small,
But until then it is you or nothing at all.
I hope we still remain friends,
Now and forever till the end.
I hate to say that love hurts so,
But it's not the love it's the letting go.
And that is what I finally had to do,
I try to be strong and let go of you.

I DOUBT WE ARE FRIENDS

We always use to talk on the phone,
Or call and see if each other was home.

You said we never stopped being friends,

That you never said it was the end.

But not talking to me is just as bad,

And even though we don't speak, I still make you mad.

Every now and then you say hi in the hall,

But that's the only word you say at all.

Like you don't know who I am,

And all the times we talked was not worth a damn.

I can remember all the things we talked about,

When we were happy, sad or in doubt.

I know things can't be exactly like it was then,

But there is no reason why we can't be friends.

WILL THINGS BE BACK TO NORMAL

I don't know how it happens how things come to be,

How things finally come to perspective and make us all see.

That everything we thought was right and strong,

In the end we saw that it was all wrong.

I'm sure you'll never forget all the fun times you had,

But some things will always remind you of the bad.

When everything is over and things are straightened out,

Maybe there will be no more doubt.

And what you two had together,

Will be in both your minds forever.

And even if you try to forget,
Things will remind you of how you met.

But hopefully for you things will turn out right,
Instead of what happened to me, just sitting by the phone every night.

Because no matter what I do it never does ring,
And again I try and figure out everything.

So now all we can do for these friends,
Is just to forget the past and start over again.

NOT A SOUND

I hate to see them walk by,
And know they'll get mad if I say hi.

Last night I waited for the phone to ring,
Thinking nothing was wrong not a thing.

That everything was like it was then,
That all of us were still friends.

But the phone never did ring not a sound,
And again I let myself down.

I got my hopes up and I said I never would,
But all I can do now is hope for the good.

It will take time that I know,
But part of me will never let go.

PAUL

You are a nice person and thoughtful friend,
Someone who's been there for me in the end.

Some people laugh or just make fun,
But you say smile no matter what they've done.

You don't care if people disagree,
You just tell me to be me.

Because there will always be people who are mean and nice,
And before picking friends always think twice.

That I have to stand up for my own pride,
To set a pace and keep that stride.

Not to let people get the best of me,
To let pieces fall soft and easily.

I hope next year our friendship will grow,
For that would mean the most to me, I think you already know.

I have learned that good friends are hard to come by,
But once you have found them it is worth all the tries.

I thank you for all the advice you did lend,
And I will always think of you as a good friend.

MY FRIENDS

Some of these people are still my friends, and that they truly are,
But others for one reason or another have drifted a far.

But for the sake of memories, which I can't seem to erase,
I would like to share with you how everything fell out of place.

So to start things off nice and slow,
I will start with the people that I had to let go.

John was so nice without his friends near,
He was always kind and full of cheer.

But when his friends would wander in,
That's when the trouble would begin.

Tim however was like a best friend,
Always there for me in the end.

But number one with his friends he always had to be,
And in the end the only person hurt was me.

Mike at first really never said much,
But as the time passed on and things changed like such.

He would say I bugged him all the time,
But that's when he found out, I wished he were mine.

That's how my friendship with him did end,
And he said we could no longer be friends.

Tracey Pizzino

Missy was someone I got to know,
And then our friendship started to grow.

I just can't believe after all I told her,
I found out she was just a user.

For Mike was her friend before I came along,
But no matter what, it was still wrong.

Russ just lets things float over his head,
He never gets involved, but listens to what is said.

He seems to be around when you need to talk,
And I can call him to go for a walk.

Roger is sweet and very kind,
But he does say what's on his mind.

We had fights here and there,
But always I knew he cared.

Ricky I have known for about ten years,
And he knows some of my fears.

For I have called him once or twice,
And he always has the right advice.

Even though he is best friends with Mike,
He does only what he wants to do and that I like.

Paul is a different story all together,
With him I could talk about anything forever.

I made one mistake and sort of got burned,
And believe you me, I did learn.

You see I use to like Paul and told him so,
But I realized I needed his friendship more and let the dream go.

But Mary is someone I can trust,
And I believe what she says and that is a must.

Everyone has fights with all friends,
But not once did we let things end.

Jenni and I have a lot of ups and downs,
And we almost always have a frown.

But we help each other see things through,
And talk about people and what they do.

So now you have it in short form,
Friendships can be strong or easily torn.

So these memories of my friends are with me to stay,
But I have to look over the past and live today.

But we all make mistakes now and then,
When it comes to sisters, brothers and even friends.

Tracey Pizzino

BEYOND ALL DOUBT

You had a friendship fresh and new,
And ever since kindergarten this friendship grew.

Something happened and you don't know what or why,
But it is at the point where you want to cry.

You are trying everything to get this friendship back,
But there is something that you lack.

To make a friendship work it takes two,
To help you see everything through.

To share the laughs, listens, and the cries,
To have the strength and the will to try.

Give it time and it will work out,
You guys will be friends, beyond all doubt.

SUMMER

Is a time to be free and play?
To put all the school days away.

To forget the homework and the books,
To try and forget the dirty looks.

To be with your friends and have fun,
To take time out to get something done.

But for me it is different in more than ways then one,
For now all I can do is remember the fun.

So when I go for my walks this year,
There won't be the smiles, but all of the tears.

I will try and see what will come to be,
Maybe the summer will make us friends again you and me.

But all I can do is hope for the good,
And pray you will talk to me I wish you would.

Maybe then we could get things straightened out,
And when the summer comes and goes there will be no more
doubts.

That me and you will be friends,
And this time it will last till the end.

FRIEND GOOD-BYE

I thought things were back to the way it use to be,
That we were really friends again you and me.

That the friendship we lost we finally got back,
But there is one thing that we lack.

It takes two people to make a friendship work out,
To help each other resolve all the doubts.

Tracey Pizzino

To share the laughs, listens and the cries,
To make sure that the dreams don't die.

To be there for each other whether happy or sad,
To try and help when we are mad.

And I'll take away the gray skies that hang over you,
And change the color so you just see blue.

But now I don't know what will come to be,
But at the moment I don't think we are friends you and me.

But if that's the way it has to be,
I won't get hurt again, I'll make myself see.

That you guys aren't worth the trouble and pain,
Because being your friend was no big gain.

Yes, we had fun times when we were friends,
But you're the one that made it all end.

So I guess I did everything Tim, I really did try,
But if you want it to be like this lets just say good-bye.

I'll have the memories of how it use to be,
No matter what happens to you and me.

I WILL NEVER FORGET YOU

I wish things could be different, but why even try,
For if you don't have two people giving then the friendship dies.

I don't know what happened for it to turn out like this,
But as for you and me having a friendship I don't think there is.

Maybe we should stop talking or just being friends,
Because they say what you have in the beginning you will have in
the end.

And before we were in the same class, we just said hi,
But you can't even say that so please just say good-bye.

For if our friendship is over, please tell me the truth,
For if that is how it will be, I'll move on to something new.

I won't dwell on the past no matter what I do,
But one thing is for certain, I will never forget you.

COUNT ON ME

I may not be there everyday, like it use to be,
For I must move on and make a better me.

But no matter how far away I may go,
There are a few things you must always know.

You have been a great friend, who's always cared,
So if you ever need me, call and I'll be there.

I have confided in you, with things no one else would understand,
I swallowed my pride and my life I put into your hand.

Though you have never let me down, never once did you lie,
You covered my back and was there when I cried.

You are more than my friend; you are like a brother too,
No matter what, you'll help me through.

We shall be friends forever, on that you can bet,
Never in a million years could you I forget.

I will definitely miss you when I do go away,
But there will come a time I'll see you another day.

I'll keep in touch, I'll write, I'll call,
I'll never let our friendship fall.

So good-bye for now, yet should you need a listener or a friend,
You can count on me until the end.

ENDS A DIFFERENT WAY

Things were always good to start off the day,
Then everything ends a different way.

Someone hurt, someone mad,
Someone happy and someone sad.

It never fails; it's always the same,
The rules never change to this game.

But it's always someone different like musical chairs,
The way these emotions are always shared.

Nothing happens the way we planned,
Nothings easy and no one understands.

You tell one person something and the rest wants to know,
You can't even believe it was said though.

But you brush it off like it's no big deal,
No one will know exactly how you feel.

But this one little incident will be filed in my mind,
Something that will definitely last through time.

But with that thought I'll end you see,
I wonder if your friends with me.

LOVE, MARRIAGE AND BABIES

BRIGHTEN MY DAY

To someone who has brightened my days,
To someone who's made my blues go away.

To someone I hope to know forever,
To someone whom I shall always remember.

We can talk about anything we have nothing to hide,
I can accomplish anything with you at my side.

My life has a new meaning, words couldn't even compare,
To the happiness I've found, because with you I share.

But there's one more thing before I go,
Something I hope you already know.

My feelings, my hopes and dreams,
And every thought that comes between.

No matter what happens in the future should it not last,
I have the memories of the past.

The best of times, I will always recall forever,
When I think of you and me together.

It's as simple as a rose, every year in bloom,
As consistent as every night in the sky's a moon.

It's the last thing I think of before I drift to sleep,
And the first in the morning before the sky does weep.

It's something I think of each day through,
The happiest times in my life, is when I think of you.

MY LAST THOUGHT

You wanted me to write a poem unique but yet,
A poem written only for you, no one would ever get.

A little something that means more than gold's yellow or money's green,
Thoughts and feelings that are so complex, you must read between.

Well here you are, this is it,
If the shoes too small, make it fit.

But not in your case, your different than many,
With a lot to say, more than plenty.

You are nice and cute, your kind and sweet,
You've got a personality that can't be beat.

You make me laugh, you make me smile,
You are someone I can talk to for awhile.

You are always there should I need a friend,
Things I say and do, you always comprehend.

You have your bad days, as I have mine,
You are a friend that I hope will stay through time.

There's not to much more for me to say,
Except I will never get angry and walk away.

I shall always stay and talk should things get out of hand,
And should you need space I will try and understand.

But one more thing I want you to know,
It's very important I tell you so.

Before my eyes close and I see skies of blue,
My last thoughts of the day are always of you.

EVEN IF IT'S NOT ME

I have always wondered when it would come,
For me to be the lucky one.

To be happy and oh so loved,
I have looked below and above.

Will my chance ever come around?
Or shall I always look to the ground.

I have great friends, who are special to me,
But when is it my time to be.

Happy and glad I have someone too,
This time I was so sure it was you.

Tracey Pizzino

But again I have made a big mistake,
But I am still your friend, by fate.

You have someone and you are happy now,
I tried to put on a cheery face somehow.

And friends with you I shall stay,
And I'll just have to wait for the day.

For when that day comes and he opens the gate,
Will it be worth the wait?

But until then I shall wonder still,
Is it worth the pain and chill?

To have someone so close and near,
And try so hard to hide the tear.

To keep on pretending again and again,
That you I only care for as a friend.

To you and everyone else that's all it will amount too,
But alone I shall think of you.

Happy is one thing I'll pray you'll always be,
Even if it's with someone else and not me.

YOUR LOVE

I am so happy that we can talk,
Maybe in the summer we could go for walks.

But just being there with you is fine with me,
For that is the place I wish to be.

For now we just talk but maybe when,
Time progresses we will be more than friends.

But no matter what happens or how long things last,
I never want to live again in the past.

So if things go wrong and it comes to an end,
I hope we can still be the best of friends.

Because losing your friendship would be worst of all,
But at least I would have good memories at times of recall.

So now I have said how I really feel,
And maybe in time your love I will steal.

Maybe my hopes and dreams will come true, And there will really be a me and you.

THERE AND BACK

I hope things are going great,
Nothing there for you to hate.

Everything happy, nothing to hard,
Just enough to keep you on guard.

I wrote about a card I would hopefully find,
Well, forget that was on my mind.

Because instead I shall write you this,
Something cheery and full of bliss.

Something only one may tell,
Something I know so well.

I shall never have to wonder how it would be,
Not to have a single friend you see.

For I know our friendship will always grow,
Not melt away like falling snow.

Because no matter what, I know it's true,
I shall always have a friend in you.

Remember that when bad times role in,
I do not run, but fight and win.

The same applies to my friendships you see,
So you will always have a friend, me.

Don't be sad for the distance between,
Be happy and proud and always dream.

For you can make anything go away,
Just dream a lot, but live today.

And for the days when all you do is try,
Or when you sit and see the clouds cry.

Just always know at each days end,
The little voices you may hear are only your friends.

Reminding you that you are anything but alone,
It's just you are there and we are home.

Just one more thing before I go,
Something you should already know.

That as much as you think about someone too,
Bet on anything she's thinking of you.

IF THINGS WERE MEANT TO BE

No matter what you do,
There will always be him and you.

You two were so very nice,
You always looked like sugar and spice.

You two were so very happy together,
I thought it would last forever.

But then they came along,
And before you knew it, you two were gone.

But if things were meant to be,
There will always be a you and he.

LET'S NOT FIGHT

I am so happy when we get along,
When we sit, talk, hear our song.

We have good times and bad times too,
That is when I feel blue.

When we don't talk, just sit there and fight,
Those are the days I cry at night.
I hope we have the best anyone ever had,
And look at some of the good things, not just the bad.

But now to you all I can say,
Is to a great boyfriend, Have a Nice Day.

WITH YOU I LONG TO BE

I am so happy when we are together,
I hope we last forever.

I hope we only have the best of times,
And the love of a special kind.

The times I see you are special to me,
But at times I wish we could be.

Close to each other night and day,
But we can't seem to find a way.

For you to come here and me to go there,
It doesn't mean that I don't care.

I hope you feel the same way as me,
Because with you I long to be.

STILL ALONE ...

We almost had what we dreamed,
You and me so it seemed.

But then one day she came along,
And I had my doubts, it was wrong.

You should not be with her but me,
And hopefully soon this you'll see.

Even though time has past,
You hopefully will be my last.

And we will have the chance again,
To be more than just friends.

For if the moment should come around,
I won't turn away or stare at the ground.

I took a risk and turned the wrong way,
But this time I won't let you go a stray.

I was foolish then, when I let go of you,
And I'm back to say, I think my love is true.

I DO

When you were little and things were rough,
You would go to mom or dad because they were tough.

Then things started changing and on your own you could stand,
You didn't need the comfort you found in their loving hands.

Then you met someone special, someone you grew to love,
Someone who encircled your world, like the sky does a dove.

You talked, you joked, you laughed, you cried,
But always stood by each others side.

No worries to think about,
Never room for doubt.

Then came the commitment, the engagement day,
With those words that hundreds even thousands will say.

And your answer was clear with each tear in your eye,
The word yes came out as you cry.

Tears of happiness, but there's something more,
Something better than before.

The date in which you two have set,
May 21, 94 we won't forget.

For that is the day my one and only sister shall stride,
Down an isle and become the bride.

Laughter and tears shall be heard through the crowd,
As we listen to each word said out loud.

Then the part will you take thee, through better or worse, in
sickness and in health,
To love and honor, in poorness and in wealth.

To always be there for one another,
To one day become father and mother.

To always stand tough, to always be strong,
To stand by each other when things go wrong.

To compromise every now and then,
To be nothing less than the best of friends.

To be prepared to give each other your heart,
To stay together till death do you part.

Then it is time for both of you,
To look at each other and say I do.

Tracey Pizzino

To my only sister, her husband, my brother-in-law, just gained,
Through the happiness and good times through the heartaches
and pain.

I love you both, and would like you to know,
My thoughts are with you, no matter how far you may go.

Congratulations is one thing I'd like to say,
I'm happy to be part of your special day.

And with honors I'd like to have a toast,
To the one person in my life that means the most.

And also to Eric, on whom I shall end,
Take care of your wife, my sister, my friend.

JULY 16, 1994

This is a special day, one you won't forget,
When everything is said and done, your vows are like a net.
Your love molded into something wonderful and rare,
Something very few things these days could even compare.
To give yourself completely, body, soul and mind,
Is something very few ever seem to find.
To say you love the other and for the other to love you,
That is what you promise on this day to do.
To look ahead together at the bright blue sky,
Yet to be right there if the other should cry.
To accept the bad days with style and grace,

To always give the other one space.
To trust each other with one's life,
To deal with the pain and strife.
To understand above all else,
To be nobody, but yourself.
To do everything together side by side all the way,
To look forward to the coming of each new day.
Yet above all else through life's little turns,
You will both, grow and learn.
That no matter how difficult the road may appear,
With the other at your side there is nothing to fear.
I would like to toast to the groom and bride,
The two of you standing side by side.
To two special people I would like to say,
How happy I am for you on this day.
Congratulations are in order, my blessings to you,
May each day be full of happiness all the year through.
May each moment be filled with memories to be told,
And all the love your hearts can hold.

TOGETHER ALWAYS STAY

What started out so long ago, as kids playing in the sun,
Continues even today, when all is said and done.

Friends from the start, which has lasted through the years,
From the good times and bad, to the laughter and the tears.

The day has come upon you, for you to take a bride,
For us to be there and watch you, walk down the aisle side by side.

For as you travel down this road, things may get in the way,
Just recall what brought you here and together always stay.

Whether times are happy or times are tough, remember that in the end,
You are more than just husband and wife, but also the best of friends.

God bless you both on this journey that you have now begun,
For September 22, 2001, Ted and Cherie, two hearts become one.

A WEDDING DAY WISH

The time has arrived for the two of you,
To walk down the aisle and say I do.

When the two of you are joined as one,
A day you thought would never come.

To say forever, till death do us part,
You shall always give each other your hearts.

To have family and friends, oh so near,
And love that grows stronger throughout the years.

Through good times and bad, to cherish and love,
May all your blessings flow from the Lord up above.

To be willing to bend for the rest of your life,
To be the best of friends as husband and wife.

Congratulations Chris and Shannon, and may you always stay,
As happy as the both of you are today.

TWO HEARTS

Through happiness and sorrow, joy and tears,
To always stand by each other through the years.

The day has arrived for the two of you,
To walk down the aisle and say I do.

To be something bigger than a sister or a brother,
To one day become a father and a mother.

You will journey together through all of life's curves and bends,
To be more than just husband and wife, but also the best of
friends.

For your family and friends shall always remember this day,
And in our hearts you shall always stay.

Todd and Leslie on June 20, 2003 when all is said and done,
Is the day two hearts finally become one.

BABY TO BE

I don't know how I will express,
The way your mother feels, but I'll do my best.

Tracey Pizzino

Nothing could have darken the day,
When she found out, you were on your way.

A month went by and things began to change,
And nothing would ever be the same.

She said I need bigger clothes that will grow,
Because I am just beginning to show.

But that did not stop her at all,
She said okay let's go to the mall.

She looked at furniture and books too,
The only thing she thought of was you.

We laughed and joked and said she looked like a tent,
But she was happy and very content.

I'll let you in on a secret though,
And it has to do with friends and foes.

No matter what she will always be,
Right by your side like she is for me.

And when the day comes for you to start school,
Homework will come first that is the rule.

In a couple of weeks we will finally see,
The baby, the person you have come to be.

But boy or girl your mom does not care,
She just wants to hold you in her arms and share.

All the love and knowledge that she does posses,
And trust me when I say, you have the best.

CONGRATULATIONS

We may have had some fights you see,
When we never thought of you and me.

We only thought of our own life,
And as a result caused a lot of strife.

Not just little spats here and there,
Words that hurt like I don't care.

But hopefully all of that is done with, through,
No more fights between me and you.

But now to get at what I would like to tell,
You my friend I hope will do well.

For when you get married and have your child,
For ahead of you are a lot of miles.

But I am sure you will just be grand,
Not because of your love or kind hand.

But if your reflect on your child, is like you as a friend,
You will be the best mother till the end.

You will be there forever, for your child to be,
Just like you have always been there for me.

But also if trouble should fall from the sky,
Please know that the relationship will never die.

And for that day when you need a friend who cares,
Just remember forever I will be right there.

So good luck Pam on your new life to come,
And you'll have Jami to remind you that you have won.

SARAH

A baby girl were you blessed,
To share fun times and clean the mess.

To have a life of wonderful days,
To cheer her up when the sky is grey.

To love her all her life through,
To be proud of all her accomplishments too.

But mostly she has given you the joy you wished for,
And God made her a girl instead of a boy.

Her life will be full and always complete,
She will be special and very unique.

For she will have fun playing with toys,
And later in life capture the heart of the boys.

But one thing she will always have until the end,
Is a person who will be more than a mother, but also her friend.

She will have problems as all girls do,
But mostly she will see all of these things through.

And she will always thank God above,
For giving her you two as parents, who she shall always love.

DECEMBER 2, 1993

The day you waited for is finally here,
A gift you will hold so dear.
A time of happiness, a time for grace,
Has been blessed to you, by a tiny face.
I may not have known you both for long,
But the feelings of love I see are strong.
You are kind and caring, always willing to lend a hand,
You always do your best to try an understand.
You have all the qualities to make the best parents around,
You have the personality that picks people up when they are down.
You laugh, you joke, and you listen and hear,
But most of all you are always near.
For the birth of a child is a great joy,
And you have been blessed by a baby boy.
Yet if you think about this in a different way,

You are not the only ones that gain something today.

There will be sleepless nights, and lots of tears,

And more than your share of worries through the years.

Combined with good times, bad times, laughter and pain,

Sunny bright blue sky days, followed by heavy rain.

All the memories as parenthood unfolds,

Plus lessons you can't learn, but must be told.

Yet through all of this, one day, it will seem so clear,

To the bundle of joy you hold so dear.

And the look in his eyes will be worth the strife,

That all kids cause their parents throughout their life.

For when the time comes for Bryan to fully comprehend,

You are not only his parents, but also his friend.

AMANDA

The days are numbered, the time is near,
For you to be almost here.

Mommy is waiting for the signs to say,
Okay, I am on my way.

Your big sister is eager to see,
Tell me mommy, will Amanda look like me.

Brie is ready to show you how things are done,
To help you with puzzles and have some fun.

The road has been long, but worth every bit,
And your mommy wanted you, she wouldn't quit.

So once again we are waiting for your time to come,
When it's your turn to be the little one.

But let me tell you something that has never changed,
The way your sister feels about you is exactly the same.

From the moment Brianna found out you were a little girl,
You somehow became her world.

And you are all that matters to her in the end,
Because she already thinks of you as her best friend.

For I hope your big sister will always be,
There for you, like your mommy has been there for me.

LOSS OF A LOVED ONE

MISSED, MORE THAN YOU KNOW

Words can't express, the loss at hand,
All of us felt, by this man.

I never had the chance to meet you, face to face,
But from everything I've heard no one can take your place.

You were more than a hockey player; you were a husband, father,
and friend,
Someone that will be cherished, always till the end.

For the people that knew you, will never get the chance to say,
How much you meant to them, and how their lives, you did
change.

So when it is time for us to recall,
We shall try and remember it all.

The good with the bad, the happy with the tears,
The fun times made, through the years.

To clarify this, we only have to ask your wife,
For you gave three children the chance at life.

To look at them, it's you we see,
This is how it's suppose to be.

Yet the one thing that cannot be taken away,
No matter what people may do or say.

Is your memory and love that is in our hearts,
And shall remain there forever, long after we part.

This is not a final good-bye, just a curve in the street,
For one day in the future all of us shall meet.

But until that day, comes around,
We must be strong and stand our ground.

There is one more thing I would like to say, and this is forever,
You shall never be forgotten, but always remembered.

Steve, you shall be missed, more than you'll ever know,
And the hardest part will be, finding the strength to let go.

WE SHALL NEVER FORGET YOU

I didn't know you and never heard your name,
But I know some friends of yours who are looking for who's to blame.

For taking their friend, caring and true,
They can't understand, why you.

I have heard of how kind you were, the loyalist of friends,
And not one of them could understand why it had to end.

Why you were the one picked, to be the one to go,
A lot of people would like the answer, but shall never know.

And no matter how hard it seems, your memory, they won't erase,
And no one could ever take your place.

We know you can't read this, for you are no longer here,
Just know to your friends you were dear.

But it didn't end with just you,
Because when you left, part of them died too.

But in their hearts and minds you shall always stay,
And that thought alone will get them through the day.

I know it won't be easy, in fact harder yet,
But I just hope you really know, you they won't forget.

And one more thing we have learned, above the rest,
God has proven to us all, he only takes the best.
    1-19-90

JASON

We did not know each other long, at least not long enough,
And I really was too little to understand all the stuff.

I know I use to play with you, that I do remember,
Me and Shannon could have done that forever.

But circumstances arise with no time to think things through,
And then away from us they took you.

Tracey Pizzino

They have always said that only a few go before the rest,
But why is it that God always takes the best.

You were so good I can just imagine how it would have been,
To not only be in your family, but also be your friend.

When you left we were sad, that I hope you know,
We begged and cried and begged some more but we couldn't
go.

I know it was a long time, before I came to see,
Where it was they took you, far away from me.

I have no reasoning for why it took so long,
I guess I needed to make sure I was strong.

Not a day goes by when I don't stop and stare,
I wonder do you know I care.

Do you remember me just a little, if at all,
Do you know if I could I'd call?

I hear your name and my thoughts come back, all good but
few,
But the time will one day come again, when I see you.

Until that time I promise you no matter what happens now,
My memory of you I'll always keep, this to you I vow.

And though reality is sad but true, I will never forget,
The love and joy I felt the day, when first we met.

This is my tribute to your memory and soul,
With all the love a heart can hold.

JUST A LITTLE WHILE

I don't know why things happen, to make people sad,
But right now things are pretty bad.

Just two weeks ago we were all talking together,
I didn't think that was it, the last time, forever.

I thought I would see you again,
And even run into you now and then.

I am really trying hard to wear a smile,
I just wish I could see you again, just for a little while.

I keep thinking who will go now,
I have to stop thinking like that somehow.

But it is a lot harder then anyone could know,
How can I rationalize this, when I can't even let go.

But please know one thing that shall always stay true,
Not a day will go by when I don't think of you.

I can normally hide the pain, but this is much stronger,
For I wish the day would come to see you a little longer.

Maybe in time I shall get my wish come true,
But until then, I will miss you.

I know you can't read this, for you are no longer around,
Just know I'll be strong and won't let you down.

GRAMMA

For the times you were with us meant a lot,
And all the little things we never forgot.

Like when you were there when we needed someone to talk to,
And never, no matter what made us feel blue.

You cheered us up when we were down,
You made us smile instead of frown.

You made us laugh when we wanted to cry,
You said never give up, to please just try.

First, you always thought of us,
And when we came over you always made a fuss.

We will never forget all you have done,
And in our minds you are #1.

Now you have left for it was your time,
But you will always be in our minds.

And even though we are now apart,
Just remember Gramma you are in our heart.

GOOD-BYE MY FRIEND

How do I do this, what can I say,
So I will feel a different way.

You were so friendly and so kind,
Yet no matter what you spoke your mind.

You listened and talked, you gave advise when need be,
We had great conversations, yeah we did, you and me.

You put a smile on my face, when there was a frown,
You always knew what to say when I was down.

I may not have known you long, but from what I did know,
Your smile and laughter will be with me wherever I may go.

You brought happiness and fun times to the people that you met,
And I hope you know that I won't forget.

From what I have seen you were loved with reason,
You were a gentle and kind as the change of a season.

Yet for all the people that love you, shall miss you even more,
Than anyone ever thought possible before.

Your cheerfulness and strength, your guidance and your will to fight,
Your lectures and your sense of humor, but most of all the talks at night.

All these things will come to mind, each time someone recalls,
The happy times and sad times when one would fall.

You were always there; ready to give a hand,
Reassuring someone, that you would understand.

I know you can't read this for you are not here,
Just know to me you were very dear.

I just wish I could have said good-bye, to you face to face,
Because everything is wrong, it seems so out of place.

I never got to thank you for always being there,
I never got the chance to let you know I care.

I never did tell you that, my friend, you'll always stay,
Even though now we are worlds away.

I'll miss you more than ever, along with the rest,
I just wonder why he always decides to take the best.

HAVING TO SAY GOOD-BYE

How can I put this, in words of the heart,
On how we saw you from the start.

So friendly and loyal, courageous and strong,
You always found the good in people, never the wrong.

You were so nice to talk to no matter what the day,
You always seemed to have something nice to say.

A great friend to those of us who knew you and those whom you
just met,
A special kind of person one does not forget.

To someone who could smile more than anyone I knew,
No matter what you were faced with, you saw it through.

With wisdom and strength, you fought till the end,
Yet now we must let you, rest in peace my friend.

To all of those who loved you, your loss, causes great pain,
But by knowing you, we shall all share a special gain.

We shall never forget you, and with each passing day,
Whenever I think of you, I shall stop and pray.
That you know how much you are loved and always shall stay,
Always in our hearts, forever an a day.

That you shall be missed more than you know,
And the hardest part will be having to let go.

From where I stood you were a great mom, sister and friend,
Someone many will never have the chance to know again.

I still don't understand when things are said and done,
How is it he always picks the best ones.

So as I go to leave and think all this through,
This is a tribute from me, in memory of you.

GRANDMA

How can I word this, so everyone can see,
This is a view of my grandma, from me.

A loving wife, mother, sister and friend,
Someone you could always count on in the end.

One you could talk to, one that would hear,
All of your dreams and worries year after year.

She loved playing cards, and her soaps were a must,
But she would have missed them for any of us.

Her thoughtfulness and caring, her happiness and grace,
Are just a few of her qualities no one can replace.

She shall be missed for different reasons from us all,
But always wear a smile, when Mary you recall.

And even though we have to say good-bye today,
Just know in our hearts, you will always stay.

UNTIL WE MEET AGAIN

How do we begin to say,
What we feel on this day.

You humor, your laugh, your friendly smile,
Knowing for anyone, you would go that extra mile.

So many are proud of what you had achieved,
You strived toward your goals, and in yourself believed.

The sadness we feel, just doesn't compare,
But in our hearts, we know you are there.

You will be missed more than you know,
And no matter what we'll never let go.

Our memories of you will continue to live,
This promise to you we shall give.

There are so many ways to describe who you are,
At least four I can think of so far.

You are a boyfriend, son, brother, and friend,
However this is not good-bye, but until we meet again.

Your time with us was not yet done,
Yet for some reason you were the one.

God chose you Steve, above the rest,
I guess it is true, he takes the best.
  WE LOVE YOU. WE ALWAYS WILL.

Tracey Pizzino

GRANDPA

What do I do, what can I say,
That will do justice for you today.

You were a great person; father, brother, grandpa and friend,
And though you are no longer with us this is not the end.

You are looking down on us with grandma right by your side,
The way is should be, even if it makes us cry.

You always were there for us no matter what or how,
Just know that we are all together for you now.

You let us get away with more than you should,
But what our parents did not know, for us was very good.

You are loved by so many, and were heroes to some too,
But in the end you were just being you.

We love you grandpa more than you will ever know,
And the hardest part was for us to let you go.

MY TIME

I don't know how to say this, but please don't shed a tear,
All of you no matter what, were always kind and dear.

Sometimes things were done or said to make the other sad,
But now we must focus on the good and forget the bad.

I don't want I'm sorry', I wonder if she knows, today,
I just want to ease your mind with a few things to say.

Don't look in the past and wish you could change,
Things you will never, be able to rearrange.

Always look forward and with the mistakes we've learned,
Know you can't stand still and wait to get burned.

Remember the fun times, when we were together,
And live by the rule nothing's forever.

And when you think of me, smile, don't cry,
For it was my turn to die.

And if a smile can't form when me, you recall,
I would rather have you not remember me at all.

But all of you know me; I try to have the last word said,
Even at a time you all do dread.

But this is not a one way street, if you think of it this way,
We all lost a little something today.

Something's are the strongest, and the toughest to make,
One person knows what I mean, yes a friendship cake.

I took all I knew and made more than my share,
But I always made sure that you all knew I cared.

Tracey Pizzino

So as I go to end this, and let you reminisce,
Being a friend to me is like a first kiss.

No matter how bad or good it has been,
You'll always remember it till the end.

So when your times are darkest and you can't shake your fears,
Just close your eyes and know I'll always be near.

Looking over your shoulder, making sure you are fine,
Because as I said before, my friendships last through time.

And so now I want to reassure you all, one thing more,
Something you have all heard a dozen times before.

One thing that's truly beyond and above,
Are the two things people can't take away from you, My Memory
and My Love.

BIRTHDAYS

WHAT ARE FRIENDS

Friends are people who know your good points and your bad,
They are there for you when you are happy or sad.

Friends are there when you need them most of all,
They are there when you need someone to call.

Friends are with you every step of the way,
Clearing the paths that once were grey.

Friends are hard to come by they say,
For a good friend can come or go at any day.

Sometimes we have a quarrel with our friends,
But that doesn't mean the friendship must end.

For I am glad to have the time,
To look at people and say you were a friend of mine.

So on this special day be glad,
Try not to let things make you mad.

But before you go I just wanted to say,
To a good friend, Happy Birthday.

TO YOU, FROM ME

Another day, another year,
Times of happiness, times for tears.

Things to think of day to day,

People to meet on the way.

Friends that may come or go,

New people you got to know.

Everything is still the same,

Nothing added to the game.

"Life's" what we call it by,

And you managed to stand high.

You made it through another year again,

But something's different this time friend.

The thing this year brought to be,

Was you becoming a friend to me.

The best thing one could pray for,

Would be to have a friend like you, behind a door.

And I opened the best door too,

And the result, I'm friends with you.

But that's only the beginning now,

I had to let you remember me somehow.

And I found exactly what I wanted to,

Yet people are telling me I should not do.

But it is more than a gift you see,

It's not just to you, from me.

Like a thank you, I like it than it's gone,

It's something like our friendship, strong.

And it shall last forever and ever,

So you can forget me never.

And when the day comes for us to go,

You can look at this and know,

I am somewhere far or near,

And my days are not as clear.

Because I had to say good-bye to you,

It's something I know I'll have to do.
But you will be thought about often and always know I care,
And any time you need a friend, call and I'll be there.
Because I think above the rest,
You my friend deserve the best.
There's one last thing about this time,
Something that comes to mind.
This is a very special poem for you I'd like to add if I may,
Cause it not only says thank you for your friendship, but Happy
Birthday.

ALWAYS THERE

To a good friend who was always around,
And to someone who never let me down.

Always there to here my sorrows,
And always there to share tomorrow.

Always there through the good times and bad,
Even there if I am sad.

Always there if I was down a bit,
Showing me the good things and saying not to quit.

But also you were there through thick and thin,
And still stayed if I didn't win.

You are a nice person but also my friend,
And that's one thing I hope will not end.

I have known you almost my whole life,
Through the happy times, sad times and even the strife.

But you always seem to be there no matter what people may say,
So to you I wish only the best and a Happy Birthday.

FOR A SPECIAL FRIEND ON HER BIRTHDAY

A birthday thought, you're one of a kind,
You always have others in mind.

You help your friends through thick and thin,
But most of all you help us win.

You don't care if we are thin or fat,
You like us the same just like that.

When I am in doubt, you're right there,
Telling me to smile, showing that you care.

I could never thank you for all you have done,
Because instead of losing a friend, I gained another one.

But now to you all I can say,
Is to a great friend, Have a Nice Day.

HAPPY BIRTHDAY

To a great sister and a great friend,
Whenever I need advise you are willing to lend.

You are there when I need you,
When I am happy or feel blue.

We have good times and bad times too,
But we always manage to see them through.

The bond between us grows stronger as a year has passed,
And hopefully this year won't be our last.

We can never know what is our fate,
But remember you I could never hate.

And if something happened and we should part,
You will always be in my heart.

I can't think of anything else to say,
Except to a great sister, Happy Birthday.

FRIENDS FOREVER

To a friend whom I just met,
But one I will never forget.

To someone who is nice and kind,
One of the rarest combinations to find.

Nothing but nice to me have you been,
And from me to you I thank you again.

You have been there when I was sad,
Always there when I was mad.

Yes, there were times when I was mean,
But friends like you are far between.

Telling me to smile if I was blue,
Always there, that was you.

So with pleasure I will say again,
I am very glad you are my friend.

And friends is how I want it to be,
Friends forever you and me.

But to get at really what I wanted to say,
I just wish you the best and a Happy Birthday.

A BIRTHDAY THOUGHT

A birthday thought, you're kind you see,
And you have always been that way to me.
Never sad or down a bit,
Always happy and full of wit.
You are kind to everyone,
And you should be proud of what you have done.

Always happy, always there,
No matter what the reason, you somehow care.
Always cheering up people, that is what you do,
Whether they are sad or very blue.
You are the kind of person I know I can trust,
And to have a good friendship that is a must.
I know if I ever need to talk at all,
You will be there when I call.
You always give me advise now and then,
And that is my definition of a good friend.
One thing I will never regret,
And that is the fact that we met.
To me you will always be a good friend,
Now and forever till life's end.
And graduation won't keep us apart,
Because all my friends are in my heart.
I will always remember the good times you see,
But mostly the fact you were there for me.
But there are two more things before I go,
One is how much you have helped me you'll never know.
The other thing I wish to do,
Is tell you Happy Birthday and say THANK YOU!

HAPPY BIRTHDAY SIS

Another year and another day,
For you have come along way.

You went through crisis of good and bad,
Days you were happy, days you were sad.

Tracey Pizzino

You set a goal for your future plans,
And you are reaching for it with both hands.

Going to school and work too,
Making good grades to get through.

You have less than one year to go,
Until you are fully in the worlds flow.

But one thing that can never change, no matter what will be,
We will always be sisters you and me.

Not just sisters, but also friends,
And always forever to the end.

No one can break the bond, for which we share,
And no one can tell us we don't care.

Cause always I will be here in time of need,
Always by your side indeed.

But I would like you to know that I am very happy to tell,
I am very proud of you for doing so well.

You have done a lot, in which some can only dream,
Yes, you have hurt along the way and made some steam.

But you always hung in there through thick and thin,
You were determined not to lose, you were going to win.

And win is something you have certainly done,
And that makes me feel as though I had won.

You are a good sister and no one can compare,
With the special love that me and you share.

So with this in mind I would like to tell,
That you my sister should do very well.

But today I would like to wish you the best,
Because nineteen years ago today this world was blessed.

THANK YOU

At first I wasn't to sure,
If the things I would say would cause a stir.

But things were fine, in fact grand,
I don't know how, but you did understand.

You listened to what I had to tell and things were fine,
And then we became better friends in time.

I can talk to you about anything now,
And you always seem to care somehow.

You made me seem happy and at the same time proud too,
And I hope you will always know I am also here for you.

I spoke my mind and how I felt,
And we dealt with the problem dealt.

So a thank you, I would like to say,
And a friend to me I hope you will stay.

But one thing please always know,
I will never do anything to hurt you so.

My friends always are most important to me,
And if I have to sacrifice myself, then that is how it will be.

So a toast to you, and above the rest,
Happy Birthday Peggy, from me to the best.

SOMETHING I'D LIKE TO SAY

This is something I'd like to say,
To a friend, on a special day.

A friend is someone who is always there,
Always around to show they care.

Always trying to understand,
There to lend a helping hand.

I want our friendship to always grow,
Not melt away like the snow.

You told me not to get you a thing,
But I did and it has no strings.

There is only one reason I bought it for you,
It's something I just wanted to do.

A thank you was not needed; the look on your face was fine,
I wanted to get you something that would last through time.

So that when the time arrives for us to be friends no more,
I will not be a face forgotten behind a door.

For when the day comes for you to recall,
I want our friendship to be remembered with a smile or not at all.

I think this gift means a little more,
Then it did when I bought it before.

And I hope you will always be glad,
And thoughts of our friendship never make you sad.

But one day the favor I'll return you'll see,
I'll be as good a friend to you, as you have been to me.

But until that chance comes around my way,
I'd just like to say thank you and Happy Birthday.

TO YOU FROM ME

I wanted to give you a present, which could only come from the
heart,
A picture, in words, of how our friendship did start.
We talked every now and then, a hi, bye, it's through,

No conversation between me and you.

Then someone said something and so the game begun,

But this game he lost and we won.

That's when we started talking more, and friends we were,

All of it started by just a little stir.

You have been a terrific friend, who's helped me more than you know,

And there are something's I wish for you to remember no matter where you go.

Number one, if you need someone to listen, advise, or a friend,

Just call and I'll be there just say where and when.

Number two, when sadness comes and your world turns grey,

Again I shall always be there, to brighten up your day.

Number three, when times are great and no one seems to care,

Call on me if you need a friend and I'll be there.

Number four, the last one, but has the same importance as the rest,

No matter how tough the roads may seem you only deserve the best.

You have listened to my problems, and have always seemed to care,

No matter how bad my day maybe, I know you're always there.

And should the time come when one of us must leave and go a different way,

I'll never forget anything, but I'd also like to say.

There are a couple of things I'd like you to remember,

No amount of miles could change the fact you are my friend forever.

I'll always cherish our friendship through the good times and the bad,

I'll always try to help should you become sad.

And I'll hope our friendship will continue to grow,

Not melt away like falling snow.

And through arguments and laughter, through happiness and tears,

One thing you can count on, my friendship through the years.

So should the world get lonely and you feel there is no one around,

There will be no need for you to frown.

Because somewhere, someplace I shall always pray,

That you are happy and safe every day.

I'll try to repay you, someday you'll see,

I'll be the kind of friend to you, which you have been to me.

So to a good person and a good friend,

There's one more thing before the end.

No matter what lies ahead of you, along the way,

I'd like to say thank you and Happy Birthday.

A SPEICAL PLACE

Something's may be spoken, yet some are never said,
Some we always hope and pray, they know what's in our head.

But why wait till the end, when one can no longer hear,
Why put yourself through wondering, did they know I loved them dear.

Well this is what I have to say, to you a special friend,
One whom I know will be there in the end.

No matter how much time passes by when we do not speak,
For those are the times I recall the memories which I keep.

Only a selected few,
Has been a great friend to me, like you.

Always there to help in anyway,
Always with the right things to say.

It's only been three year since we've met,
But with a lifetime of memories I could never forget.

So as another one of your birthdays arrives my friend,
I'd like to remind you of something again.

No matter how far, no matter what comes to be,
You shall always have a friend in me.

No matter what's said, or what time may bring,
I found a special friendship that has no strings.

You have always been helpful; you have always stood strong,
You never walked away, when things went wrong.

You are more like my brother, yet one of my best friends too,
And I always care and worry about you.

But most of all I would like you to know,
No matter how much rain, or how deep the snow.

I will always have a special place in my heart and mind,
Where no one can touch, no one will find.

A spot for only your friendship and how much it means,
No one will ever be able to come between.

I wish you all the luck and in case you don't remember,
I love you and you'll be my friend forever.

So on that I'll stop and say one thing more,
Happy Birthday Mickey, may it be better than before.

OCTOBER 14, 1993

A birthday has arrived, time to stand and cheer,
Do I hear a celebration, please pass the beer.

Another year survived, another year has passed,
I don't know about you, but I hope it's not the last.

To someone always willing to sit and lend an ear,
To let me complain about things, that very few will hear.

To try and understand, instead of saying I'm right or wrong,
For being a great friend to me and staying strong.

Because you made me feel part of something, not many tried to do,
But most importantly, just for being you.

I guess it's not how many friends one person has got,
But the quality of those friends, which means I have a lot.

The good times may be few, but good none the less,
So on your birthday Scott, I wish you all the best.

Tracey Pizzino

JUST THREE WORDS

Another time, another place,
Things just left without a trace.

Things that once was very strong,
Somehow now seem so wrong.

What really happened, no one can tell,
Maybe that is just as well.

From the best, to not talking at all,
From long conversations, to hardly even a call.

From hello, how are you, everyday,
To not even one word do we say.

Yet we are still friends in our minds,
Something that won't change with time.

It's hard to believe, it's sad but true,
No more fun times between me and you.

It's like a stream that lost it's sparkle and glare,
Something that's no longer there.

But through everything I still hang on tight,
To the hope that one day it will be right.

The memories keep me going, plus the good times we had,
And I do my best not to be sad.

But something's change and we have no control,
Not even when it comes to our heart and soul.

"A friendship cake" I made and will always remember,
The great times we both had together.

You, my best friend, for so long,
Have taught me how to be strong.

To fight until the bitter end,
To always stand by a friend.

To know when to back away,
To be able to think but not say.

I hope things are fine and you are doing well,
Also there's more I'd like to tell.

But time waits for no one, and it never stands still,
So with a lot of courage and strong will.

I wish you the best birthday of your time,
This is from me, to a dear friend of mine.

Though words don't say everything and good-bye says to much,
I'll just end this with three words, Keep in Touch.

Tracey Pizzino

A WORD SAID SO FREQUENTLY

A word said so frequently, yet no one seems to care,
That just using the word, does not mean it's there.

The word I am referring to is "friend" you see,
And this is the difference between them and me.

I do not use it carelessly, like every time I say hi,
I do not say everyone I know is my friend, why.

A simple word, yet so complex, the meaning ever changed,
From something good and special then totally rearranged.

For it takes a certain quality, that makes one a friend,
Someone to share the good and bad, and cry with now and then.

Someone who can see your flaws and like you all the same,
For someone who is always willing to talk before placing the
blame.

To put their problems away, just to help you out,
For that is what friendship is all about.

Sure we may have acquaintances, people we see now and then,
Yet truthfully looking close enough, do we have that many friends.

People that will stick by you, no matter what may be,
Someone who is in a bad situation, yet the good they only see.

To take you at your word, to believe what you say,
To always have faith and never walk away.

Friends start out as strangers then a word is said,
And in front of us we start to pave the road ahead.

Through curves and hills, valleys and planes,
From something so understandable, to almost insane.

No matter what the reason, people that come and go,
Only a handful can be called friend this we always know.

Sure they may hurt us more often then not,
But their help and kindness we never have forgot.

So as I go to end this I would also like to say,
I hope you have a great time on this special day.

And may all your dreams somehow come true,
Because in my book, the way I see things, "a friend", is you.

NO AMOUNT OF GOLD

How can I put this, what's there to say,
To write this in a different way.
To do it better just once more,
To say it differently than before.
To say how I feel about things right now,
To take an oath, say a vow.
To make you understand the actions and why,
At times it is so hard I try.
To make you see again and again,

That I am still very much your friend.

To pray and hope that you always know,

No matter where it is you go.

My biggest fear, for something to go wrong,

When one of us is no longer strong.

To know in my heart as well as my mind,

That our friendship will last through time.

Will you always know how much I care,

And if I could, I would be there.

To help out or just listen for awhile,

To talk, cry or walk a mile.

To understand the situations and the way you keep things in,

To always stand by a friend, even if they don't win.

To never let you down, I'll always try my best,

To stop trying to make everything one big test.

To always know when to go, to turn around and leave,

Not to bug you as much, but help you to achieve.

To know my limits, this promise I make,

I will never be a friend who's fake.

I won't pester you all the time, or call everyday,

I'll never tell what's always wrong; I'll tuck it most away.

This year has passed leaving behind memories good and bad,

Times that we were oh so happy and times when we were sad.

But the good out weighs the bad by far I will admit,

And no matter how high a mountain may seem, I promise I won't quit.

This friendship has seemed longer, and I hope it will stay,

As strong and as good as it is today.

I hope to be your friend forever that's one thing I will tell,

And I also wish you well.

No more proving anything, nothing to be told,

Because I've found a friendship worth more than any amount of gold.
Have a great birthday and just in case I'm not around,
It's easier to walk through life with a smile, then to wear a frown.

A BETTER FRIEND

We told each other once before, never would we say,
Something that we wanted to hear just to get us through the day.
To never lie or compromise our friendship at hand,
To try our best to listen and to understand.
To never try to cover up what the other said,
To always be able to say what's in our head.
Well as you know the above has ended, we broke each and every one,
But it is something together we both have done.
We may have said some choice words because of anger, but then,
We talked it out between us two and we still are friends.
We may not always agree on things because we are to much the same,
But for anything that happened before, I accept half the blame.
We have to learn to work together, to trust each other too,
So we are there no matter what the other may do.
To also know how the other one acts can sometimes be a gain,
But to make this friendship strong again, is to me worth the pain.
To know if something goes wrong, in me, you can confide,
Because with me there is nothing you need to hide.
I promise to be a better friend then I was to start,
I promise to take all my knowledge and combine it with my heart.
To always try to be around should a problem occur,

To know when my part is done, to never cause a stir.

I will not bug you like before, I've learned my lesson from the past,

Just because we may not talk everyday, doesn't mean our
friendship won't last.

I apologize for everything that I may have said or did,

I have to start treating my friends like friends, not a little kid.

To let you make choices on your own, and still stay by,

No matter if I approve or not I simply won't even try.

I'll accept the answers with the reasons and never doubt you see,

For that is how it all started between you and me.

Once you start to doubt, things go downhill all the way,

And even with a second chance you don't know what to say.

I know it will never again, be like it was before,

But we have the chance in the future to make it so much more.

So to someone who has put up with me from day one on through,

I only wish the best of luck, to my friend, you.

May all your days be happy and all your nights be bright,

May all the choices you ever make always turn out right.

May we never argue like it was in the past,

May we try everything to make our friendship last.

But through all the fights we have the good is what I like to recall,

For those are the best memories of all.

And though another year is over an another stares us in the face,

I hope you know my friend; no one can take your place.

And all of which is why on this special day,

I'd like to wish you most of all a terrific Birthday.

THE PERFECT GIFT

Here we are once again,

Spending another birthday with a friend.

I may give lectures, and advise here and there,

And bitch more than a little, but it's because I care.

I can tell what is wrong, by the look on your face,

Or tell when something is fine, everything in place.

We talk and we don't, we laugh and shed tears,

But that my friend will go on through the years.

You are more open now, then you were before,

You are opening everyday, farther that door.

Sure we have bad times, but all friendships do,

The only thing different with me and you.

Is at times we may hurt each other to bad,

And do nothing to fix it and we are both sad.

Yet most of the time we see the hard times through to the end,

And come out of it ahead, as better friends.

So I may not know exactly what the perfect gift is to buy,

But I can give you something, not seen with the human eye.

It won't fade away, as the years come and go,

And it will never be able to wash away with the melting of the snow.

It won't mold or spoil, it will never tarnish at all,

It will never laugh or make fun if one day you fall.

No one will ever be able to take this away,

No matter how much we fight or what we should say.

Some will only laugh at this, and some have never understood,

When you find something special, you hold onto it for good.

The memories, the laughter, the talks and the fights,

The "whys" and the "what ifs", the crying at night.

The understanding, the helpfulness, the loyalty too,

Everything I've ever done was because of you.

To my best friend and brother whom I've known for years,

I shall never forget the good times, never regret the tears.

And in case you haven't guessed it, the gift I've already gave,

It's something in your memory, I hope you always save.

The memories of the good and bad, and the one thing that is true,

Now and forever, my friendship, I give to you.

No matter how long our lives maybe,

No one can take these memories from me.

And until I'm buried six feet under the ground,

If you need me I will always be around.

And even if I'm not, just close your eyes and know,

No matter where I am, no matter where I go.

I'll always hope you're safe and I'll always care,

Even if for some reason I can't be there.

So Happy Birthday Dave, on that I will end,

You are a special person, you are my best friend.

A BIRTHDAY WISH

We may not always get along,

But one thing I know our friendship is strong.

You have always been there when I needed a friend,

And for you I'll be there again and again.

Never think for a minute, you are all alone,

Just because of the fact you are far away from home.

For you are in my thoughts each day,

And things will work out somehow, someway.

We were always there when the other one was in need,

But there's nothing I can do, for on this war they feed.

On the hearts and anger, the hopes and dreams,

And everything that comes between.

We can't let them win, no matter what they do,

For I must hold on tightly to a friend, you.

I wish things were different then they are now,

I have to be strong for you somehow.

And though things may sometimes seem dim,

Just think positive and you'll win.

There are so many things I would take back in a glance,

But the past is past, the present is now and the future is one big chance.

But as a friend to you, one thing I won't let happen ever,

No amount of miles could change the fact you are my friend forever.

So as I go to end this, there's one more thing to say,

I shall always pray for you at the end of each day.

Happy 21st Birthday Ricky, from me to you,

And I have all the faith in the world, you'll make it through.

Thank you for always listening and always seeming to care,

But thank you for most of all just being there.

MISCELLANEOUS

M.M.I.

Well let me see how I will start this one,
Because it won't consist of anything I have done.

It will be mainly of the way I feel,
And the friendships to me that I thought were a steal.

My life has been a long curvy lane,
With a lot of good times, and also some pain.

I always have the problem of following my heart,
Even though that is not so smart.

This can cause troubles in more ways than one,
Because a lot of times you will lose just when you thought you had won.

I have been so blind to what's in front of my face,
And because of this things fell out of place.

I convinced myself the more you have the better off I'd be,
But instead I found out it just wasn't for me.

No one can help me; this is something I must do,
I have to follow my head for once and find out what is true.

I have to set aside my feelings and do what is best,
Then maybe finally I can easily rest.

So I can stand on my own two feet with nothing in the way,
And if I concentrate hard enough I'll get to that point one day.

But even though this maybe something for me to do alone, which is kind of hard to do,

Cause even though I said I will do it on my own, you are part of it too.

Always there through bright blue skies,

Even when the clouds start to cry.

Advise for every problem I have, no matter how hard it seems,

Whether you know it or not you are a big part of my dream.

I am the one, who thinks things through,

Of what I say and what I do.

But you carry out my every thought you see,

And in case you don't know whom I am talking about, this poem is for me.

And no matter if friends stay or even say good-bye,

Three will remain forever; they are me, myself, and I.

MOM, WITH LOVE

Moms are put on earth to show us the way,

To tell us right from wrong each passing day.

They are here to help us grow,

To turn us in the right direction and painfully let us go.

To help us find our life, as they have found their own,

And yet they are still there when we smile and groan.

For our birthdays and first dates they have never forgot,
And to us that means a lot.

Even if we argue or even disagree,
You always seem to be there for me.

To help me with problems or just sit and talk.
Every once in awhile we even go for walks.

Mom, I know you will be there for me till the end,
Because you are not just my mom, but also my friend.

DAD

When we were little and would take a nap,
While we were sitting on your lap.

When we fell, you picked us up off the ground,
When we needed to talk you were always around.

No matter what, you were there,
Helping us in anyway showing that you care.

If we get hurt by one of our friends,
You are always there in the end.

And when our hair turns grey with curls,
No matter what, we're your little girls.

Tracey Pizzino

And if something happens we can count on you,
To help us see things through.

But no matter how far apart we may become,
Just remember dad, you're #1.

So on this 21st of June be glad,
Because you are the best in the world DAD!

A PROTECTIVE SISTER

I wish I could tell you how sorry I really am,
For everything I said and ever planned.

I don't know why I do things as much as I do,
Maybe I am just mad at you.

I hope you will forgive me for all I have done,
Because you lost two friends all because of one.

I don't know what to do anymore, but I know one thing for sure,
If it takes me the rest of my life I am going to cure.

The two friendships you have lost,
All because of this one cost.

So open your eyes and see,
All this happened because of me.

A Protective Sister

THINKING OF ME

I sit here and think of things that I hope will be,
When it is all hope, not reality.

I sit in my room at night and wonder if he is home,
But then I give in and pick up the phone.

My fingers start pushing the numbers I know so well,
I have so many questions and things I would like to tell.

But I don't want to be foolish and risk something good,
But the little voice inside says I should.

Talk to him about it all,
And just be careful in case I fall.

But then I sit here and think what will he say,
Will he hang up or just walk away.

Will he just forget about the friendship we had,
Look at me, laugh and get mad.

Tell me! Why do I sit here hoping of what could be,
When I don't even know if he's thinking of me.

Tracey Pizzino

OLD TRICKS NEW SHOES ALL YOU JERKS ARE STUPID FOOLS

They say you forget, that time heals,
But they never told us about the deals.

The little tricks that you think of a lot,
The ones that make you say I forgave and forgot.

Because the people that hurt you once, always hurt again,
And they make you believe they are your friends.

Then the times comes to tear down that wall,
The one that protects you so you don't fall.

At times they talk so nice to you,
But then something was said and it has to be you.

All the pain, all the fights,
They threw it out the window that night.

They lied and showed me their true soul,
They are no better than fool's gold.

Fake as ever no matter what they said,
As far as I am concerned they are dead.

They put me through hell once, nothing can change that,
They talked about me to my face and others, stabbed me in the back.

I feel this time I have finally learned,
That dealing with jerks will only get you burned.

So now they have to get out of trouble themselves,
Because I put them where they belong, back corner top shelf.

And if they would like to sucker me again,
They have a very long wait my friend.

Because I wanted them to know I hate them more than ever,
I wanted them to remember one last thing forever.

And that would be to look them all in the face and ring a little bell,
And before I turn to walk away say, "I hope you burn in Hell"!!!

JUST BLACK

I wonder would you not talk to me if I was the one shot,
Would you just look and say you deserved what you got.

Would you understand why my friends did not come around,
Could you comprehend their parents thinking next their kid could be down.

Would you think I was bad for being at the wrong place at the wrong time,
Or would you love me just the same and try to ease my mind.

All I can do is wonder what the answers would be,
Because you are thinking of just what you hear and see.

I know you love me, no question there,
But if you love me as much as you say, please just be there.

Because my friends to me are just people too, and to me that is that,
But my friends to you are not my friends their just black.

33766 OR 53666

I can't keep it straight you see,
Was it 33766 for me.

Maybe it was 53666 for you,
Well as we both can easily tell neither one it true.

They are just numbers we use to talk,
We don't need invisible ink or chalk.

Our little secret, no one else knows,
A little something we did alone.

I think it's you, you think it's me,
Neither of us won, cause it wasn't meant to be.

But one thing forever we can dream,
Are 33766 or 53666 with you or me.

I also looked at the phone one night,
I came up with 7258 246634 and it's right.

STEPS OF AN ADDICT

This is how I think it goes,
The first step is to just say no.

The second step you hesitate more,
The third step is the word "yes", you open the door.

The fourth step you can't seem to get enough,
The fifth you would do anything to get the stuff.

The sixth step you take just a little more too,
The seventh they shut the lid on you.

That's when eight comes, your friends crying,
The ninth, them thinking, did they see you dying.

The tenth step is me, every shape, form and way,
The eleventh step would be to have you here today.

The twelfth and thirteenth step is different you see,
That's when step one in turn becomes step three.

You are classified as an addict to whatever you did chose,
But in the end, my friend, you lose.

Maybe you were lucky and are still of the living,
But you are doing anything but winning.

I have tried to help you, but it's not the same,
You must do it for you, and on yourself place the blame.

I just hope when the day comes to say I told you so,
I'll say it to your face and not a casket under snow.

THE HEARTBREAK KID

You set a goal for yourself 18 years ago,
Yet through all the anguish and the pain you would not let it go.

You strived for every match you won, and then in the end,
All the hard work and practice paid off my friend.

For you have something only a few can say,
And it happened March 31, 1996, we won't forget the day.

You became the WWF Champion; your goal had come true,
Now everyone is asking, what will Shawn do?

Defend your title, yet through it all,
You have dished out some holds and took some falls.

But no matter how long it took, or how much pain,
You have done something only the elite can claim.

Through your career you have held not just one, but three title belts,
And yet you always are trying to better yourself.

Well it doesn't get much better than it is right now,
But always remember this saying or vow.

"A winner is not someone who never fails",
"A winner is someone who never quits".

This fits you in every shape, form and way,
And now I will end this with one last thing to say.

For all you are going to do, and to everything that you did,
Congratulations Shawn Michaels, A.K.A. "The Heartbreak Kid".

OCEAN

The birds fly, the water roars, the sun shines so bright,
Yet when dark falls it's just as lovely, the moon glimmering at night.

The one place that's so peaceful I can dream whatever I want too,
And with the magic of the ocean, I know it will come true.

From the sand sifting through my toes, and the vast amount of space,
The memory of this scene could never be replaced.

Time seems to stand still, yet nothing stays the same,
For if I blink my eyes, I've lost it, with no one to blame.

The wind seems to come from nowhere, and then becomes so still,
It seems to have a mind of it's own combined with power and will.

The sense of belonging is so powerful and yet,
There is a certain mystery deep within it's depth.

The one I can count on no matter what the day,
The ocean will always be there, it will never go away.

For when I need it I can always depend,
On a good listener, the ocean, a forever friend.

BELIEVE

Through wins and losses, fights and goals,
The story of champions starts to unfold.
The tunnel was dark, then light shown in,
The season everyone thought you would win.
Then the loss, what do you do,
Learn from this and move on through.
Another season with one goal in sight,
To prove as a team you will stand up and fight.
And that you did every step of the way,
That is what got you here today.
Through all the heartaches, pain and tears,
Finally it came, that day, that year.
Head held high, cup in hand,
Saying this is for you, the fans.
Boyhood dreams finally coming true,
All of it was done by you.
You are the ones, who went through all the strife,
With your friends, girlfriends, families and wives.
The glory that came that one bright day,
One week later was taken away.
From tears of happiness, to tears of despair,

Just know good or bad I will be there.
As a team you went to war,
And came out closer than before.
You are teammates, but more important friends,
A bond that will be strengthened in the end.
Whether Stanley stays here where he belongs,
Or finds a new home when the season is gone.
No matter the score, or what the outcome may be,
You will always stay number one to me.
For Vladdie and Sergei you are always in my mind,
My thoughts and prayers I hope you will find.
Not a day goes by that I am not proud for what you have achieved,
And in my heart I will always believe.

LIFE LONG FRIEND

I hope you are happy today,
Cause there are a few words I'd like to say.

This may be a little late I know,
But just be patient, cause here I go.

We have had some fun times in the past,
A couple of bruises here and there but they didn't last.

All of them were good times, not one bad,
I can't recall you ever making me sad.

I did not know what to get you; I was stuck at the start,
I had to figure out something special, something from the heart.

Well I finally found it; it's not much to see,
But it's a symbol of how I look at you as a friend to me.

Someone that's always happy, and willing to take the time,
To listen if something is on my mind.

Who never takes sides, stays neutral to the end,
And somehow manages to be to both people a friend.

You can call it silly, maybe dumb too,
But this is how, I see you.

So Merry Christmas Gary, and thank you once again,
And I hope forever you stay a life long friend.

CHRISTMAS 1997

This is it, the last one,
So we have to do stuff we have not done.

Things that we can remember,
Things we can do one more time together.

For after this Christmas there is only 5 months more,
Than we have to say good-bye and open a new door.

Not let go and forget the past,
Because the memories and our friendship will always last.

This may be the last Christmas for awhile,
But we can always send letters to make the other smile.

You may not like things people do,
But that is just because you are you.

As you can see I really don't mind,
Because you are best friend I'll ever find.

So for this last Christmas again,
Just except these gifts and be happy friend.

I'll explain each gift one by one,
And maybe you'll understand what I've done.

The car is to show the dreams we've had together,
So you can remember the good times forever.

The necklace is a sign of our friendship in heart,
And how it has grown since the start.

The teddy bear will show how I see you,
Understanding, caring and happy too.

And the gold bracelet shows through all the strife,
If you don't have a good friend, you don't have a life.

But most of all above the rest,
It's because you my friend, deserves the best.

Tracey Pizzino

MERRY CHRISTMAS

Another year has come and gone,

And yet our friendship is still strong.

We may not talk all the time, and yet,

We know if we need help the other is there, on that you can bet.

I tried so hard to think of a gift that would suit you,

But no matter what, this I could not do.

What do I give a friend, who has always been by my side,

To someone who doesn't let me quit, when I felt my hands were tied.

And sometimes you would try to make me understand,

That at times it was my fault for problems at hand.

But a friend to me you have always been,

And I would like to thank you again.

I have no idea how I deserved a friend to be,

As good as the kind you have been to me.

And I never thought of the perfect present to give you,

But when I saw this rose bud I thought of you.

For you have come a long way,

And had a few blue skies turn to gray.

But you kept fighting until you won,

And I am proud of you for what you have done.

So please accept this rose as a knew start,

And know it only comes from the heart.

So now it is time to part, but before I go,

I would like to wish a Merry Christmas, to a friend I know.

And a good friend you have always been to me,

And I'll return it to you, one day, you'll see.

CLASS OF "88"

Some of these friends we have known through the years,
And we have told to our hopes and fears.

They will remain in our minds,
Because friends like these are hard to find.

We stuck together like we were one,
And all the things this class has done.

All the little things that meant so much,
Like the good times, prom and such.

For when we started four years ago,
But now it is time for us to let go.

Of all the things that meant the most,
So with the parting of friends we should toast.

Maybe we will meet one another again,
But we will have all the memories till then.

Of all the snow days and when it would rain,
All the heartaches and the pain.

But now we have made it to the end,
And have to start over again.

We will cry and shed some tears,
But just remember the good times in the past years.

Be successful and full of spunk,

And be glad you didn't flunk.

Good-bye Robichaud, teachers and friends,

Until we have the chance to meet again.

But the past four years have been great,

And I wish all the luck to the class of "88".

THIS DAY

To someone sweet and very kind,

Someone that helped me ease my mind.

This day belongs to you and no one else,

For you have managed by yourself.

A little help you had on the way,

But for the most part it was you who made this day.

We all pray and wish it to be,

Then when it arrives we can't believe what we see.

It has appeared a lot sooner then some of us thought,

But now it is time for the class of "90" to part.

But for me to have you as a friend,

Is one thing I shall have to the end.

The way we became friends is different you know,

But I am also glad it happened though.

We both managed to help each other when a problem appeared,

You helped me make grey skies clear.

For you have helped more than you could see,

And I hope I have been the kind of friend to you, that you have

been to me.
But because you are going to school in a few months now,
There is something to you I wish to vow.
I vow to you on this day,
I shall never let our friendship stray.
I vow to also always be around,
To make sure I never let you down.
To be your friend through good and bad,
To try to help should you become sad.
And above all else I would like to add if I may,
I am very proud of you today.
So as I go I would like to wish you well,
And there's one more thing I'd like to tell.
No matter what happenes, I'll say it again,
To me you will always be a special friend.

GRADUATION DAY

You never thought this day would come,
After all the hard work was done.

It was tough at certain times,
But you kept fighting and things were fine.

Now and then you were sad, for you were alone,
Because of the fact you were far away from home.

A congratulations is in order too,
Because even after the obstacles you came through.

With flying colors, but most of all,
You kept on fighting even when you would fall.

Now you can rest for a few weeks too,
And be around the people who have missed you.

Again congratulations from all of us here,
And always know we do care.

We are proud of you, we must say,
So have fun and a great graduation day.

ALONG THE ROAD

Your graduation day, has finally come,
A way to show everyone all that you've done.

You made it through school, though it may have been rough at
times,
But you never gave up, and for the most part things went fine.

Well now ahead of you is a whole different way,
To live and survive in the world today.

Along the way you'll keep your old friends, plus make some new,
And remember there is nothing that you can't do.

Just take it one day at a time and everything will turn out,
Even though along the way you'll have 100 doubts.

It may not be easy and things will definitely change,
And the way we spent our time, we'll have to rearrange.

You won't be able to talk to your friends like you did before,
Because now the time has come for you to open a new door.

Things will never be as they are now, maybe never again,
For everyone is going their own way, the people we call friend.

But there is no point in dwelling on what's going to be,
Just concentrate on only what we can see.

So I hope your day is happy, and your future bright,
And I hope everything for you, only turns out right.

You will definitely be missed and thought about too,
And I hope you remember that no matter what you do.

For all you have accomplished, I am proud to say,
How happy I am for you on your graduation day.

CLASS OF "91"

Well here you are once again,
All of your foes and friends.

Today's the day it ends and starts,
Taking and adding some to one's heart.

Never again will it be as it was before,
You will never again open that classroom door.

Tracey Pizzino

The halls you all knew so well,
Will always hold the secrets you never did tell.

Maybe one day you shall meet again,
And be able to call each other friend.

And remember all the snow days and when it would rain,
Plus all the happy times followed by pain.

Though many of you may cry and shed some tears,
Just hold onto the good times in the past years.

Think of the things you have all done together,
From fighting, to laughing, to saying how's the weather.

Plus, just be successful and full of spunk,
And be glad you didn't flunk.

For your time has come for you to go,
To live and laugh, to love and grow.

To leave behind everything and everyone,
The friends you partied with in the sun.

Never again will you all be in the same place,
Yet, still no one could take the other one's place.

You'll always remember each other as you do right now,
And in that final moment, you'll all say "the vow".

I'll keep in touch, I'll write, I'll call,
I'll never let our friendship fall.

Well it is finally over and graduation is gone,
The moment you have all been waiting for so long.

So to everything you have accomplished and as a group done,
I wish all the best to the Class of '91'.

YOUR GRADUATION DAY

When you leave, I will be blue,
But it is something we all must do.

But just because you leave for good,
We won't have to stop being friends, but if we should.

Stop talking for some reason at all,
I will miss you if you don't call.

For being your friend I was glad to be,
You made me feel happy and let me be me.

Around you I did not have to put on an act,
You were there no matter what and that is a fact.

I will miss you more than words can say,
And I don't want it to arrive, your graduation day.

You will always be in my heart,
Even if we are miles apart.

I could never forget you, for all the gold in the world,
Not for money or even a little black pearl.

I could never forget you, even if I tried,
Even though you kept up your lies.

For you have helped me through the good times and through the
bad,
You were there to help me if I was sad.

I hope you have fun in the things to come,
And conquer things one by one.

I hope you meet nice people anywhere you go,
But please don't let old friends go.

For if you feel sad for leaving your friends, please don't cry,
Just promise me you won't say good-bye.

JUST A THOUGHT AWAY

I may not have known you that long,
But for what I see you are strong.

You give your best at all times,
You never quit until the answer you find.

You have always helped me, you were never mean,
Friends like you are far between.

Your thoughtfulness, your kindness, your personality too,
All those things make up you.

Whenever we were down, had no energy at all,
You'd be there to pick us up each time we would fall.

You'd tell jokes, you'd listen, you'd also give advise,
Whenever we needed help, you never thought twice.

You have worked hard for your accomplishments, though
sometimes it was rough,
You proved to yourself through anything you can still remain
tough.

The fun times will be remembered; the bad times taught us too,
But most of these past five years you gratefully made it through.

Your time with us is over, but your friendship still remains,
Through happy times and sad times, through laughter and through
pain.

You set a goal for yourself and reached with both hands,
Some can only dream of, yet some don't understand.

So for everything that has happened and is still yet to come,
Just always know that in our hearts, you'll stay number one.

Never hold back anything; never compromise your heart,
Always know it's somewhere a good idea must start.

Tracey Pizzino

So whatever your future brings, all we have to say,

Is we're proud of you, the best of luck and HAPPY GRADUATION
DAY!

ABOUT THE AUTHOR

Tracey Pizzino has been a certified pharmacy technician for 14 years. She has received her Bachelor's degree from Eastern Michigan University and is now working on her Masters of Science Administration at Central Michigan University. She has been writing poems since the ninth grade as a hobby.

Printed in the United States
138287LV00003B/1/P